THE ETERNAL RAGPICKER

Nicos Hadjicostis

THE ETERNAL RAGPICKER

Essays on the Human Condition

Nicos Hadjicostis

Bamboo Leaf Press

To my soulmate, Jane,
triumphant over the impossibility
of living with me.

Book title: *The Eternal Ragpicker – Essays on the Human Condition*

Book Editor: Daniel Burgess
Proofreading: The Red to Black Editing Company
Book Interior and Cover Design: Poppy Alexiou
Printed and Bound: Sheridan

ISBN 979-8-9901447-1-2
eBook ISBN 979-8-9901447-2-9

Published by Bamboo Leaf Press, London, UK and New York, USA
www.bambooleafpress.com

Book cover image: Treasure Frey, *Life of Things*, 2010, Pen, ink, gouache on tea-stained paper, 13 x 16 inches/33 x 40.6 cm

Contents

Introduction

Most of the essays in this book were written between 2016 and 2022, and sent out to my bimonthly "Tuesday Letter" subscribers. Their main ideas were formed earlier in my life, and some existed as first drafts in my diaries for many years. Philosophical in nature, they explore aspects of the human condition with the aim of encouraging the reader to ponder upon them and relate them to everyday life. Therefore, they could be aptly classified under the narrower heading of "practical philosophy."

With the help of my insightful editor Daniel Burgess, we grouped the essays thematically into five chapters and then ordered them in a harmonious way to give the illusion they are somehow connected. Well, in a sense, they *are* connected, even if each essay stands on its own: their interconnectedness is not only a result of the author's language and style; there is also a *sequential* connection. For example, under the heading "On Expanding Our World," I begin with the defining essay of what exactly I mean by "expansion," which is followed by "Leaping into the Unknown" that explores the first necessary steps for such an expanded life. Once we do leap into the unknown, we discover new "Parallel Universes," and then more "Infinite Microcosms," thereby further expanding our world before we start self-reflecting and examining our own mental apparatus in "Our Compartmented Mind."

A final note on the last chapter, "On Time": our existence is *in* Time, but also *of* Time. Time permeates everything we *do* and everything we *are*. Therefore, although these essays may initially seem quite unrelated to the rest, they may end up being the most relevant of the lot to our everyday life and the way we place it within the grander context of Being.

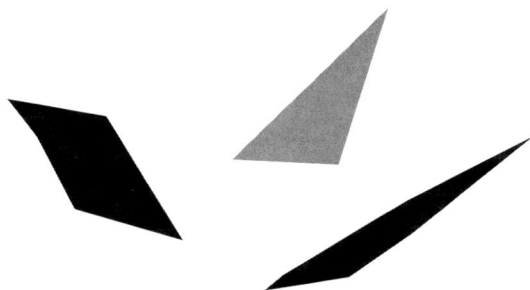

On the Nature
of Man

The Incompleteness of Man

Look at an animal—a cat, a cockroach, a fish in the ocean. All have everything they need. All are already everything they *need to be*. Animals are born complete.

There is nothing to be added to a fish or a slug from the moment it is born until it passes away—only size and mass. The day the slug dies, it is the same slug it was when it was hatched—only bigger and fatter and more unpleasantly slimy.

But Man, the human animal, belongs to a category of his own. He is born with a body not yet fully formed, helpless and completely dependent on others for more years than any other mammal. But his physical incompleteness is just the beginning. Even after he grows up—two decades of acculturation and education later—he still feels incomplete. And he struggles for completeness—be it finding *meaning, harmony*, or *fulfillment*—for the rest of his life. That's part of the *definition* of a human life: it is always incomplete.

An animal, being born complete and remaining so throughout its life, is always ready to die. Thus, there is nothing cruel in this Nature of the devouring and the devoured. Everything killed and consumed is already complete and thus, in the truest sense, ready to die. A human, on the other hand, being always incomplete, is never ready to die. It is this underlying feeling of incompleteness, still present even at the final moments of dying, that lies at the very heart of our constant fear of death. Not even a person in extreme old age lying on his deathbed feels ready to leave this world: the about-to-die feels deprived of the opportunity to complete his being before departing. This is also one of the main reasons that we have created systems of philosophy and religion: to explain, or even *explain away,* death. The eternal life for Christians, the Muslim concept of Jannah, the Hindu and Buddhist beliefs in reincarnation, are all (in part) attempts to come to terms with the fact that death may strike at any moment before we experience the fullness of life. Religions, at least in their outer forms, transform the incompleteness of Man at the point of death into a promise for completeness in the afterlife.

We arrive into this world incomplete, go about our lives searching half-blindly for ways to complete ourselves, and, in the end, after failing in our struggle, we depart with the same or nearly same sense of incompleteness as the one we had at the very beginning. What is the purpose, then, of this lifelong "struggle for completeness" when our tragic failure is preordained?

The answer to this is to be found in the word *struggle*—not in completeness itself, which is unattainable. Our struggle for completeness moves and governs our growth so that we flower into something different from what we originally were. Unlike the slug, the old man on his deathbed is not the same person as the one who entered into the world. He is *another being.* Our sense of incompleteness drives our movement towards learning, creativity, growth, wisdom. It is pertinent that the life cycle of the butterfly (and other insects, for that matter)—one of a few animals that goes through physical and other transformations throughout its lifetime—symbolizes the stages of human life in so many cultures: we are all born as caterpillars, crawling and searching blindly for food. Then one day, after we become "big and fat" (with knowledge and experience), we start eating our own bodies and turn into a chrysalis—as we grow, we unwittingly become transformed. Finally, we acquire wings, leave the cocoon, and fly—departing from this world not as caterpillars, but as butterflies.

Our incompleteness is both our curse and our blessing. We are cursed to ceaselessly struggle for completeness. But we are also blessed with the potentiality, and most often with the final actuality, of gaining wings to fly. Unlike the rest of the animal kingdom (bar butterflies!), we have the ability to become a different organism, a different being from the one we were at birth—even if we still feel incomplete.

We are the seekers, the warriors of the unattainable!

Our struggle for completeness never ends. But it is through this struggle and because of it that we are, or rather *become*, humans. For our species is not born—it is made. Or rather, it is constantly *in the process of being made*. Man is changed and transformed throughout his life. Therefore, he can never be defined—he is ceaselessly redefined through living itself. Our incompleteness becomes our only unalterable feature. We are the *permanently* incomplete species.

Restless.

Always moving. And searching. And struggling to fly.

The Restlessness of Man

Enough with the settled life!

There is no settled life—do not fool yourselves.

Restlessness is the default state of Man.

When I was younger, I used to divide people into two categories: the settled and the restless. I put myself in the second category and hated my self-categorization. Deep down, I did not like my restlessness. I saw what seemed to be the peace and calm of others, and I wished to be like them. I was surrounded by so many who were settled: those who gave the impression that they had found the answers to life's big questions, or who had concluded that these answers couldn't be found, or who were tired of seeking and ended up content to simply lead a life of everyday concerns.

In contrast, the more questions I seemed to be answering, the more questions kept appearing. And, unlike Hercules facing the Lernaean Hydra, I could not even use a torch to burn them. I was being devoured, consumed alive by the multiheaded restlessness at the center of my soul.

But recently I have revised my ideas. I have wondered for decades: Are the settled truly settled? Or is there a deep unsettledness in them? My naive dualism has now been replaced by a "Vedantic monism":

well, the settled are not actually settled! They are as unsettled as the restless. Just as the little black dot in the center of the white figure in the symbol of the yin and yang, the seed of restlessness lurks within the presumably settled.

So what happens to the old dichotomy? Are there truly no settled and restless? Am I, the restless, the same as that person opposite who seems to have dealt with all the big problems of life that torment my soul? Well, we are not the same. But our difference is not as I used to believe. We are both restless, but we deal with our restlessness in different ways: the "settled" put their restlessness "under the mattress," so to speak, while the restless confront it head on. True, many settled are unconscious of their restlessness, but others are not. It is rather a choice; they choose not to bring it to the forefront of their lives, not to make it the central issue of their daily concerns. So they cover it with other things that appear to be more important, or they pretend that those other things are imposed upon them from outside forces over which they have no control. Yet, the restlessness persists in the background.

If you think you are settled, think again! The easier it has been for you to achieve your supposed state of rest, and the more you repeat to yourself that you have settled, the more you unconsciously struggle to hide from your view that little black dot of restlessness in the midst of it all. There is no permanent settledness in settledness. Humans, as we have already addressed, are the permanently incomplete species, and therefore permanently restless. At the heart of this restlessness is none other than the fact that we are born incomplete and need to work for our completeness throughout our lives.

Heraclitus defined the nature of the visible world with the three words *ta panta rei*, which translate roughly to "everything is in motion" or "everything flows." Ever since, science has continually confirmed this truism. Rest is not a real "state of being" in the universe of which we are a part. Everything we consider as being at rest, or quiet, or even empty, is actually teeming with activity. An atom at rest is one around which electrons incessantly rotate, and the proton, once thought of as stationary, is actually a multiplex of many particles, exchanging energies in restless activity. Even the emptiness of space is replete with radiation, particles, and many other physical entities that scientists continue discovering to this day.

Just as the physical universe is permeated by an infinite restlessness, so are the plant and animal kingdoms. Nothing is more relevant to our discussion than the apparently passive and restful seed that begins to stir and break open the moment it is planted and watered. The seed's "restlessness" is none other than the seed's creative energy, the force that will guide it through its many metamorphoses so that it may become the bush or the tree. But if we could rate or calibrate all the various forms of restlessness in our universe, none would surpass the creative restlessness in Man, a restlessness that molds, transforms, and modifies matter and energy, creating objects from the mind and imagination. This inner restlessness of the human soul, which is none other than the seed of incompleteness at the center of man's psyche, cannot be extinguished. Every seemingly settled state is but a small interval on the path of a neverendingly ascendant restlessness that seeks, discovers, moves forth, and grows. Behind all human evolution, all human creations and achievements, everything we admire and strive to emulate, every great work of art, music, literature, philosophy, and science, every transformative collective struggle, be it revolution, war, or a social movement, is the restlessness of Man.

The settledness that is the result of a life that has not faced its deep questions and passions, its tsunamis and fiery volcanoes, is not a true state of rest or peace. It is artificial. *You cannot skip restlessness to find peace!* True peace and settledness are none other than the reward of a restlessness responsibly faced. Calm and peace do not come about by searching for peace for peace's sake, nor by chanting "om" all day long, nor shrinking back from the difficult external and internal challenges that Life presents us. Achilles's triumph comes on his deathbed, and Odysseus's peace comes after a lifetime of trials. Socrates's master teaching, the *Phaedo*, is given at the very end of a life during which he heeds his restless "daimonion." The Buddha achieves nirvana once he foregoes the settled life of his father's palace and ventures into the struggling world; Jesus's resurrection comes only after his crucifixion; Arjuna's gloom is lifted once he faces his restlessness and enters the battle. Beethoven's Ninth Symphony is created after he loses his hearing; Picasso's *Guernica* is inspired by a horrific war. To paraphrase Victor Frankl's idea, which he uses in another context, "settledness cannot be *pursued*, it can only *ensue*."

Restlessness is the beginning, middle, and end of peace: the *way* to it. Those who avoid facing the inner restlessness, those who fear change, those who move and act within the familiar and the comfortable, betray the essence within Man. The modern obsession with relaxation and fighting stress is completely misplaced. Granted, our modern lifestyle produces unhealthy and negative stressors, which may be termed the "surface stress" of life, and which may be handled using some of these methods. But the default stress, the *existential stress* that lies at the core of our being and makes us seek completeness and self-fulfillment, the struggle to become what we are meant to become, is not only healthy and necessary, but must be consciously acknowledged. The restless know this and harmonize their movements with this natural flow of things. That's why I sometimes feel that, paradoxically, the restless end up being more truly settled than the seemingly settled!

If you count yourself among the settled, it's time to stir things up. You are, whether you like it or not, a member of the restless tribe. Accepting, embracing, facing, and dealing with our inner restlessness is none other than an affirmation of our innermost nature as incomplete human beings. The moment we think we are self-fulfilled or done with our struggles, Life unbalances us once again by toppling our newly apparent settledness. Verily, only with Death does true rest finally arrive.

The Wave-Nature of Man

The people you meet are not really human.
They are not even material bodies located in space and time.

People are waves.

A human being seems to be, most prominently, a physical object, a body with arms and legs, a beating heart and breathing lungs. Yet once you interact with or form a relationship with one of these bodies, it suddenly takes on a different hue. It is not the original body with which you came in contact. For the relationship remains after the person departs: the image of him, the sound of his voice, even his smell, have not disappeared from your consciousness. His *presence* extends beyond his body and mind, which are now invisible. The person continues to "touch" your being in some mysterious way. Over time, you discover that the connection is ever-present, and since it operates at a spatial and temporal distance, it partakes of the nature of a wave. Even more, if the connection, the relationship, is a wave, then both of you must be waves too: for what behaves and interacts as a wave (and resides in a dimension other than that of physical objects) *is* a wave—an incorporeal form of energy or entity.

Even if we assume that a human being is a physical object as well as a wave, the wave aspect of his nature ends up being more important with respect to the totality of his life. This is so because our physical encounters in space and time are but a small subset of the much larger world in which our overall interactions as waves occur. You may have thirty friends of whom none are with you at this moment. Yet you are connected to them by invisible wave-ripples that are constantly alive: in your mind, heart, and imagination, i.e., in this larger world that transcends the physical, your friends are always present and affecting you—consciously or unconsciously.

And of course, *you* are a wave.

Being a wave, you crisscross thousands of other human waves throughout your life. And every wave has a big or small effect on your movement, on your life, on who you are becoming. All human waves are in constant motion: some come for a while and go, others stay for years and then leave only to return again, some others cross your path briefly and then vanish forever.

You are immersed in a sea of human waves.

But unlike material objects, whose movements can be predicted with relative certainty—throw a stone and you can calculate its trajectory as it is pulled down by the earth's gravity—these human waves act and behave in mysterious ways. You never know what a person will do: his decisions are uncertain, his actions unpredictable, his moods volatile, his mental health precarious, his physical presence in your life contingent upon a myriad of factors. Your relationship with another person is free-moving, incalculable, ungraspable. Like a wave, a person's frequency, amplitude, or speed may change at any moment: the indifferent neighbor may become a new friend; a loving bond may turn sour; the energetic and passionate may become enervated and slothful; the dull and boring may suddenly become creative; the ignorant, wise; the coward, brave. This fickleness, fluidity, or rather the *constantly shift-*

ing frequency of human behavior, is similar to the uncertain states in which elementary particles exist in quantum mechanics. Heisenberg's Uncertainty Principle most certainly applies to the actions of people as it does to the wavelike behavior of subatomic particles!

But people are not waves just because human relationships transcend matter, space, and time. Nor just because the overall unpredictable behavior of human beings pertains more to that of waves than to that of matter. They are waves because of another important reason: human waves extend along a continuum and therefore have neither a beginning nor an end. You may think that your first encounter with a human wave who has just crossed your path is the *beginning* of your relationship to it. But it is not so. The wave was already moving before it interacted with you. Your having met at a specific juncture in time, rather than being the beginning of anything, demonstrates the *crossing* of two waves already on a fixed trajectory. The specific circumstances that led to the first encounter were prefigured. The human wave was *already* moving in your direction before it crossed your path. This motion towards you was actually an indication of the covert connection you had already had with the other wave *before* the first encounter.

It is because we are waves that we are connected even before we meet!

We may actually think of every interaction of human waves as akin to "a momentary materialization" of two waves, similar to the collapse of subatomic waves into matter (the moment we observe them) in quantum mechanics. When they interact, when they cross one another, human waves seem to become material, gross, involved in human bodies at a specific place. But just as in physics, this is not a permanent state; this bodily encounter in the gross physical universe will not last for long. The people will part one way or another, sooner or later. Then they will go on behaving as waves. Their memory, feelings, and imagination will be henceforth interacting with one another, even if only occasionally. Therefore, the connection formed will remain influential in their lives, because its effects can never be annulled. In this sense, their connection will continue forever.

Furthermore, it is because we are waves that *every interaction we have with every human being is also monumental!* When we examine even the so-called insignificant or passing encounters in our life, they often, upon further scrutiny, prove to have also been monumental: you may have missed the train because of a quarrel you had with a train official. In the next train that you board, you meet the love of your life, your future soulmate. You may later on in life forget all about the quarrel that led you there, yet you owe the most important encounter of your life to that now-forgotten annoying official who delayed your departure. You do not remember his face, nor what the quarrel was about, but this apparently imperceptible human wave (the train official) was actually a tsunami that greatly changed your life.

Lastly, because we are waves, everything we do—our works of art, our human constructions, our acts of courage and love, our ideas and poems and songs—are wave-ripples that remain even after we pass away. The bodies and minds of Shakespeare and Beethoven have vanished, but the ripples of the waves they both *were* are still with us, influencing our lives today.

Our Wave-Being extends in the past way beyond our birth, and will extend forever in the future after our bodily death. In this sense, we may also claim to be, as much as all waves are, immortal!

All of us are waves of energy and movement and feelings and thoughts, incessantly pulsating, interacting, crossing one another, coming and going, seemingly appearing and disappearing, but never truly ceasing to exist.

The Uniqueness of Man

The thrushes sing as the sun is going,
And the finches whistle in ones and pairs,
And as it gets dark loud nightingales
In bushes
Pipe, as they can when April wears,
As if all Time were theirs.

These are brand-new birds of twelve-months' growing,
Which a year ago, or less than twain,
No finches were, nor nightingales,
Nor thrushes,
But only particles of grain,
And earth, and air, and rain.

— Thomas Hardy, *"Proud Songsters"*

❖ ❖ ❖

Out of the undifferentiated substratum of quarks that make a few different types of atoms, out of a few different chemical elements, everything springs forth. A myriad unique individual entities appear and begin inhabiting this huge expanse of Space and Time that we call the universe. And everything, absolutely everything in this universe, is unique: every pebble on the beach, every blade of grass, every plant, tree, insect, worm, every reptile and mammal, every human. And each and every one of these unique existents appears in its unique form, and in the unique evolution of its form and in the unique activities and expression of its being, only once in the universe. And it will never again appear in the universe in the exact same manner, or behave, act, express itself in the exact same way. Each existent of creation, past, present, and future, is an *absolute* uniqueness! For each existent was never before created in the exact same form it came-to-be, and will never again be repeated in this exact form. Even if it were magically to appear in the same exact form, at some different time in Eternity, still, its *activities* would be different and immersed in a different world. For every movement, every activity of every animate and inanimate existent is also unique. Every stone that rolls, every tree leaf that now sways, every insect that buzzes through the air, every animal that hunts for food and mates and raises its offspring in every corner of the planet, is acting in a unique manner that has never before happened in this exact way and will never again be repeated.

And, of course, *you* are unique! You are a unique expression of the Creation. A unique convergence of circumstance. You are one of the *latest productions* of the universe. A fresh, brand-new creation—just like the birds of Thomas Hardy in the poem above. There may be myriad others on this planet, indeed on other planets in other solar systems and galaxies, but none are like you. Even if all your qualities are shared by others, yet *all of them together*, in this special form, combination, character that constitutes your makeup, are a unique composition that has appeared here and now for the first time in the history of the universe. Let others place you in all sorts of boxes: blonde, female, young, athletic, disciplined or undisciplined. *You are one of a kind.* A category of one. A unique creature formed of inanimate and animate elements, the product of the biological and historical evolution of mankind, of the cultural circumstances that caused your being to spring forth out of nonbeing. That you exist is a miracle. That your existence is unique is an even bigger miracle.

Truly realizing your uniqueness is mind-blowing! A great wave of *responsibility* overwhelms you. You are this unique being that is called to think, act, move, create—in short, *be*—in your own unique way. You have the ability to express your uniqueness in extraordinary ways that have never before appeared in the universe. You may consider this to be a kind of calling to which you may or may not act responsibly. What are you here for? Why has Nature endowed you with these unique specific qualities that you have? What are you to do with them? These are the central questions of life. How you respond to them will reveal to you what I have come to call your life's main highway. All else is trifling.

But some may assert that the ubiquity of uniqueness makes it commonplace, and therefore there's nothing special about it. Just as all grains of sands are unique but commonplace, so too is there nothing necessarily special in being one of the myriad human beings that have existed or will come to exist. Our uniqueness, by being "a natural given," and in a sense self-evident, *in and of itself* does not make us anything special. It is simply a quality of every existent. In a nutshell: if your *uniqueness qua uniqueness* is shared by all others, it is nothing special.

Well, as it happens, this argument hides a logical fallacy rooted in language itself: the categorization of things into a group by common quality does not make each of these things identical to all others in the group. Four and eight are numbers but that does not make them the same. Their quality qua numbers is simply a prerequisite for us to compare them and make meaningful statements about them, such as eight is larger than four, or four plus eight equals twelve. We could never compare, say, a number to a color: ask which is bigger, a four or brown?! It is a prerequisite to categorize before we are able to compare things and talk about them in a meaningful way. The fact that we all belong to the category of "unique" does not make us "the same." You are unique just as each number is a unique member of the family of numbers, and just as each color is unique yet belongs to a spectrum of colors. The abstract concept of uniqueness does not annul the real uniqueness of Being. Your uniqueness qua uniqueness, just as your humanity, is shared with all other people and constitutes the common template upon which you are called to differentiate yourself by creating your own unique path. We could even go further and suggest that we should be humbled by the fact that uniqueness qua uniqueness is not unique: you are unique, just as each and every other human is unique.

Of all the hymns to the uniqueness of Man, my favorite is one by Yogi Ramacharaka. In it, he imagines a spiritual guide taking someone on a cosmic tour of the multiple physical and spiritual planes of the universe:

"But," continued your guide, "beyond your plane and beyond mine are plane after plane, connected with our earth, the splendors of which man cannot conceive. And there are likewise many planes around the other planets of our chain—and there are millions of other worlds—and there are chains of universes just as there are chains of planets—and then greater groups of these chains—and so on greater and grander, beyond the power of man to imagine—on and on and on and on, higher and higher to inconceivable heights. An infinity of infinities of worlds are before us. Our world and our planetary chain and our system of suns, and our systems of solar systems, are but as grains of sand on the beach."

"Then what am I—poor mortal thing—lost among all this inconceivable greatness," you cried. "You are the most precious thing—a living soul," replied your guide, "and if you were destroyed the whole system of universes would crumble, for you are as necessary as the greatest part of it—it cannot do without you—you cannot be lost or destroyed—you are part of it all, and are eternal."

You are not a "poor mortal thing." You are a most precious, special, and unique creation. Express your uniqueness in the most extraordinary manner you are capable of.

The Glory of Man

The sound of the violin in Beethoven's Violin Concerto leaps out of its harmonious position within the whole in order to exalt both itself and the orchestra to the heavens. In no other musical composition does a single instrument elevate itself to such perfection. It is as if the violin were waiting for Beethoven to express what itself was striving for centuries to express in order

Beethoven's Violin Concerto performed by David Oistrakh.

to reach its self-fulfillment—to individuate. This concerto is the violin's telos. The violin manages in the end to surpass the orchestra—the unus mundus, the substratum, the undifferentiated—from which it springs forth. It represents the ultimate glory of the Individual: the single voice, the unique voice, the differentiated melody that stands alone, albeit in constant relation to and dialogue with (concerto) that from which it arose.

For all this and more, the violin in this concerto is the symbol of Man. In the same way that the single melodic line of the violin both fulfills and surpasses the grandeur of the orchestra, Man too, whether he knows it or not, struggles to simultaneously fulfill and surpass the grandeur of the universe in which he finds himself. His life's struggle, symbolized by the lone melodic line of the violin, is none other than to perfect himself and at the same time harmonize his thought and action with the whole existence that envelops him. In those few perfected individuals like Socrates or Lao Tzu, we can see that Man may aspire to both fulfill and surpass the Universe, or, if we were to use a religious/spiritual language, his Creator, by transmuting his finite, time-bound, constrained single life into a Finite Perfection.

But why use the word "surpass"? Isn't that hubris?

On the contrary: it is exactly because Finite Perfection is reached in spite of and through limitation and constraint of form that it constitutes a higher perfection than the already existent Infinite Perfection. When the perfected Man attunes himself to the Infinite Divine "Music of the Heavens,"[1] and through his individual melodic lifeline reaches Beethoven's violin in Beauty, at that exact moment, by reaching the Divine from his finite launch pad, he *surpasses* the Divine. The paradox exists only because we are condemned to express thoughts within the confines of Time and the very limited terms afforded by language. For the truth is that this "achieved" Finite Perfection is already *prefigured and contained* in the Infinite as a potentiality—yet still, its actuality necessitates Man.

Jung's idea that God needs Man in order to become conscious of Himself can here be remolded into the idea that *God needs Man in order to raise Himself higher than Himself.* The Ultimate Glory of God is achieved through, by, and because of Man. It is only because Man's Finite Perfection *surpasses*—due to its apparent self-inherent finite in-

---

1 A more expansive term alluding to the ancient philosophical concept of the "Music of the Spheres" or "*musica universalis.*" According to this theory, which originated in Ancient Greece and was later developed during the Renaissance, the movements of all celestial bodies obey mathematical laws of harmony just like music.

ability to do so—Infinite Perfection that the Infinite can be *truly* Infinite. For a true Infinity is one that also includes an unending number of Finites—or as the Indian mystic-philosopher Sri Aurobindo said, an infinity of possibilities. And a Perfect or Ultimate Infinity is one that includes an infinity of Perfect Finites. Hence:

Man's ultimate glory is none other than God's own Ultimate Perfection.

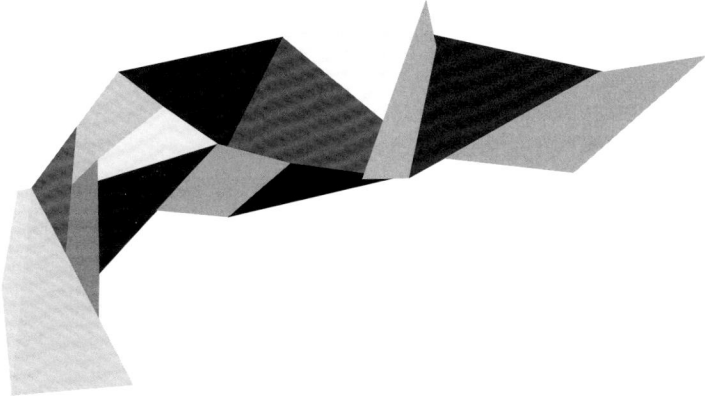

On Expanding
Our World

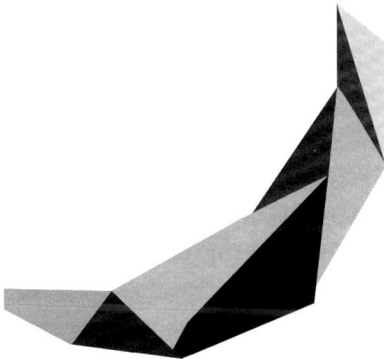

At How Many Points Do You Touch Life?

The number of points at which you touch Life and the World is *the measure of the wealth of your life.*

People ask themselves, "Are my days rich? Do I have a rich life?" But what they should actually be asking is, *"At how many points do I touch Life?"* For the "richness" of a life is proportional to the extent to which this single life touches the totality of Life and the grander World in which it is immersed. To discover where we stand with respect to this question, we may break it up into a number of more manageable parts: "What is the field in which my life moves? How extended is it? Does it have rigid borders or is it open?"

Open! That's the first concept of importance. For openness is the measure of our willingness to go beyond what we already know in order to touch Life at new points.

Openness is also the acknowledgement of the fact that irrespective of how wide and extended our present world is, it is still small, restricted, limited, and limiting.

Openness is an attitude we hold with respect to everything that envelops our being but have yet to explore. It is the attitude of opening our arms to embrace the unfamiliar, the alien, the baffling.

But openness alone often becomes passive. The world beyond

our own does not meet us while we idly meditate on its unknown features and wait "for something to happen." We need to make a voluntary movement towards the world. And this is none other than *active curiosity*. It is this curiosity that moves us towards the new and unexplored. If openness is the willing attitude, curiosity is the willingness acted upon. It is movement and action towards those spheres of Life and the World that lie outside the sphere we already inhabit. Active curiosity moves us towards new sensations—sights, sounds, smells—new people, new countries, new ideas, new books, new music, new fields of endeavor. It is the power that expands and enlarges our world.

But still, openness and curiosity together are not enough—for they may still remain on the surface. We may try listening to opera for the first time and quickly decide it is unappealing or even unpleasant. Or we may try eating durian and stinky tofu in Asia and immediately reject them because of their repulsive odors. Similarly, we may reject a new idea because it is alien to our mental world. The ears that have not been cultivated to "discover" the beauty inherent in opera; the nose that is not accustomed to discerning the deliciousness hidden underneath a seemingly repulsive smell; the mind that has not been trained to see the world from an utterly new angle, will soon resign from any effort at expansion and revert to the known and familiar.

However, if openness is the proper *attitude* for moving outward to meet the world at more points, and if active curiosity is the *movement* that makes it possible, there is a third element that turns it into reality: equality. This is the catalyst that allows us to *truly* touch the world at more points without reverting back to the familiar. There is equality with respect to our perceptions and our ideas. With respect to our perceptions, equality is the attitude and activity of forcing our senses to experience everything in its raw form without any interference from the analytical and judging functions of the mind. Quoting from my book *Destination Earth*:

Yogis have been practicing equality towards all sensations for thousands of years. The idea is to capture the *rasa*, the substance, the existential quality of each and every sensation, without the mind immediately superimposing a judgment on it. All sensations are equal as sensations in as much as they are variations on an infinite spectrum of sensations. … By forcing our mind to stand back, we may return to the primal mode of experiencing our world, like a newborn, who sees and feels everything with a freshness and intensity, unblemished by the clouding of mental judgments.

It is not easy to smell a foul odor and not react in disgust, or make the characteristic involuntary grimace. Yet it is only by refraining from reacting in this way that one may experience the foul smell in an unmediated, direct manner.

Capturing the *rasa* means that, suddenly, the foul smells in the countryside outside a remote village in India—where trash has been scattered around indiscriminately and there are no garbage collection trucks—cease to be that "single disgusting odor" that you could not bear. You begin to discern myriad shades of odor, each with a completely different assault on your sense of smell. Exploring these intentionally, then, becomes an enjoyable game. Actually, you soon discover that bad smells are much more interesting than good ones! For example, perfumes comprise aromas from a limited number of essential oils, such as jasmine, rose, and lavender, which are blended together. But bad odors are infinite, because nature creates "cocktails of stinkiness" through the endless combinations of disintegrating matter both organic and inorganic! Exploring the *rasa* of the Indian countryside surrounding the remote village, you find yourself moving inside a newly discovered *grande parfumerie* of previously repulsive odors that have now become lovingly explorable by your nose, by virtue of the fact that they are novel and strange and interesting and belong to a universe of odors that you never knew existed.

Similarly, with respect to ideas, equality simply permits us to approach new concepts with a welcoming attitude: we seek as much value in new ideas as we already recognize in established ones. Although not all ideas end up having an equal value for us, it is the approaching of all ideas with equality that will allow us an unbiased evaluation of their worth.

Equality has the sound and hue of something neutral, but it is actually a great destroyer! It destroys all labels, all past conditioning, all limiting mental vessels. Suddenly, opera is something that has beauty and I must search hard to find it; durian is a great fruit (after all, millions of Asians adore it), and I need to discover why this is so; and, from another angle, the Buddhist virtue of compassion may not be very different from the Christian conception of love.

Equality also destroys all of our irrational identifications: Why do we remain attached to the same football team from childhood? Or the same political party, the same automobile brand or fashion designer? Why do we only watch one genre of film or only American movies? Or listen to one type of music? As soon as equality begins to destroy all of these "historical identifications," all of the old loves we have grown accustomed to, we find ourselves in a much grander world of new possibilities and innumerable surprises: we start supporting another team, joining its football club and making new friends who wear different shirts; we exchange our car for a bicycle and start going to work via the forest, discovering amazing new flowers on the way; we begin listening to Chinese music, watching Japanese movies, eating Mexican food. Consequently, our life begins to touch Life and the World at points we never knew existed—or, if we did know, we had never touched! We discover that next to our own familiar universe—this little world with its own specific sensations and mental pleasures, its own terms and names, aims and desires, loves and repulsions—there lie innumerable other parallel universes.[2]

---

2   See the essay "Parallel Universes" on p. 47.

40

Openness, curiosity, and equality refer to our *relationship* with Life and the World, and how we go about touching them at many new points. But where do we stand with respect to our *capacity* to do so? What the figurative term "touching the World" actually means is *embracing* many more aspects and elements of Life and the World—*truly* making them part of our own world, not simply touching them while keeping ourselves at a distance, as if they still remain part of some other world. Embracing is integrating that other world into our existing world. It is only when the "other" becomes "ours" that we *truly* begin to touch the world at new points and enrich our life. For this to happen, our instruments must acquire the ability to truly grasp the new. It is not just a matter of magnitude, i.e., of the *number* of points at which we touch the world, but of the *quality* of our touching too—how deeply we can delve into these new points. This brings us to two very important qualities that every person, as the subject of experience, must work on in order to expand his or her capacity to embrace more fully the world: the cultivation of one's instruments and the cultivation of one's willpower.

The cultivation of our instruments refers to how equipped we are to understand, appreciate, explore, and finally embrace the world that lies beyond our own. Our senses have to be trained and cultivated in order to become refined. What we discern with our eyes, ears, and nose depends on how well we have trained them. The trained ear knows that there are hidden harmonies and melodies in many musical masterpieces and learns to discern them more easily than the untrained one. The trained nose of the wine-tester can distinguish tens of aromas in a sip of wine, which the average person cannot. Yet what distinguishes the cultivated from the uncultivated instrument is simply the effort and time spent cultivating it.

The whole field of raja yoga has developed ways to keep cultivating not only our perception but also our attention and mental concentration. Of course, cultivating our instruments is actually *not* something mysterious to be found only in yoga. We all do it throughout our upbringing, in school through early adulthood. Yet, at some point exactly there—in early adulthood!—many stop working on this cultivation, thinking there is nothing more to cultivate. But this could not be further from the truth. Irrespective of how cultivated or refined our senses and mind are, their ability to expand is limitless. Although, as Kant showed, our senses and mental instruments delineate the limits of our grasp on the world, these limits may still be considered limitless as long as we expand the ability and sensitivity of the instruments! Each time we expand their ability, they can contain more of the world within them, even if that newly contained and expanded world is still limited.

Finally, we have the cultivation of our willpower, which, in the present context, is none other than our conscious effort to touch the World at as many points as we can. In order to achieve this, there has to be both an exertion as well as a persistence to keep trying to expand our world and our field of Life. The operatic soprano voice with its strong vibrato will sound unnatural to somebody used to listening only to pop music, just as the long and windy sentences of Proust may seem impossible to follow for someone used to reading light novels. Yet, with effort and multiple attempts at grasping what we originally have failed to grasp, we are finally rewarded with many new worlds to explore and enjoy. Just as with most of our valuable gains in life, touching both Life and the World at many points requires effort and real work. However, no other work is more fulfilling than that which expands our world and our being.

Moving outward to touch Life and the World at many points, embracing fields and spheres of Life and the World that lie outside our present life, but also cultivating our instruments and exerting our willpower so that we may constantly expand our ability to do so—all of these create a life with no limits, a life richer than anything we have ever imagined.

Leaping into the Unknown

Nothing holds greater power in our life than the Unknown.
The Unknown pulls us towards new life experiences, new knowledge, new human relationships—a renewed and revitalized life.

The Unknown always calls us, and we can respond either by ignoring or acknowledging it. It may be a simple call, such as following a strange animal sound at night, trying that durian or stinky tofu, or replacing a daily practice with something novel. It may be a larger call that requires us to change our life: depart from our country, change our job, embark on a bold adventure. Or it may be the highest call of which we can conceive: the search for meaning and purpose in our life, or the search for God. Whether big or small, the Unknown beckons us to move forward, explore new behavior, touch Life at new points, connect with the ground of our Being. By moving within the field of the known and familiar, we stop learning and developing; by moving towards the Unknown, we expand and evolve.

Yet many fear the Unknown. There are many reasons for this fear: evolutionary ones rooted in the ingrained archetypal fear of predators—either animal or human—lurking in the dark; psychological ones rooted in our love of well-established routines; social ones related to our sense of belonging and our need to conform to group behavior;[3] existential ones having to do with the fear of encountering the light after getting used to living in our Platonic cave. Still, in spite of this fear, the lure of the Unknown is unmistakable in our life. We may push it aside for a while, we may pretend it is not there or deny its existence, but its call, in any of its many forms, keeps returning. The restlessness at the core of our being cannot allow us respite for too long.

Still, this fear of the Unknown gives rise to a ubiquitous defense mechanism that causes many to remain idle or even completely immobilized in the Known: many say they are willing to explore new possibilities in life, or to move into new fields of creativity and activity. Yet, because of fear, they try to find these new ways of living while remaining enmeshed in what they are already doing. Standing with one foot on the Known, they grope with the other foot in the darkness of the Unknown so that they might find a point from which to make their next step. In other words, they supposedly want to be moving towards the Unknown while still being busy reaping the fruits of the Known. But this is not how Life works.

The movement towards the Unknown requires that the Known be left completely behind.

Just as the adolescent boy must leave his mother's bosom to become a man, or, to use Kahlil Gibran's great simile, just as "alone and without his nest shall the eagle fly across the sun," the power within the Unknown is only released after we fully and fearlessly surrender to its mystery. The nest is warm, comfortable, and safe, but one cannot become an eagle without making the huge leap into the air to test one's wings in the vastness of the unknown, frightful sky. The Unknown does not reveal its gifts unless we relinquish all contact, all attachments, all footing on the Known.

---

3   For more on conforming to group behavior, see the essay "But Everybody Does It" on p. 96.

How could it be otherwise? The Unknown obtains its nature through its contrast to the Known. If we could first define, or explore, or understand the Unknown while standing on the Known—in order to get the Known's "approval"—the Unknown would cease to be unknown. Actually, there is no way to know the Unknown until *we meet it on its own terms!* It is *through* and *by* those terms that the Unknown releases its inherent power. Just as the sky only offers the abundant gifts of flight and ethereal freedom to the young eagle *after* the bird completely leaves behind the nest he was raised in, every Unknown that stands before us in our life *demands* that we completely relinquish our footing on the Known. Once we do that, every Unknown reveals itself in all its might and grandeur. The only way to learn to fly is to spread and flap your wings in the air; the only way to learn to explore new places is to leave your home and start exploring; the only way to begin a new life is to begin it.

These statements are not tautological. Moving into any Unknown is an *act*. And this act is different from the endless "thinking about," "planning," "preparing for." Such *apparent* actions are the equivalent of a hapless eagle merely daydreaming about his first flight. Such daydreaming is the main reason why many people fail to move into the Unknown: they think they may plan it, prepare for it, get to know it first while remaining where they are. They even begin to invent "the conditions" the Unknown supposedly requires of them so that it may come to meet them. But all this tossing about, all this supposed preparation, is none other than a self-deceiving game they play with themselves in order to cover the inherent fear of the imminent leap.

However, there is nothing to fear; the Unknown must be embraced. Everything that belongs to the Known of today was once Unknown. So the Unknown is just the name we give to the experiences and knowledge we are yet to gain. Meditating on how we once feared today's Known because it was Unknown and how irrational these past fears subsequently proved to be, we realize that our present fears will soon be proven equally unfounded.

The Unknown is the great silent force that has been moving our lives since birth. It is its lure and power that helped us grow and become adults, that gave us all the knowledge we have, that created the wonder and magic of the great flight of the eagle that is our life.

Parallel Universes

We live in a world of parallel universes.

The universes of politics, cooking, fashion, music, parrots!

Many years ago, I decided to buy a macaw. A few weeks later, I found myself immersed in the "world of birds." I began to discover this already existing world that was running parallel to my life but of which I had been unaware.

Before parrots, I was immersed in the world of chess. For some time, my world was that of Karpov and Capablanca. A big part of my daily life was learning chess openings with weird names like the King's Indian, the Hedgehog Defense, and the Fried Liver Attack. I studied chess books, met people who played chess, and traveled abroad to participate in chess tournaments. So absorbed was I in the chess world that people in my dreams began to move like chess pieces: diagonally like bishops or hopping around like knights![4]

---

4   When I first read Stefan Zweig's famous *Chess Story* in my youth, I thought the dreams of his protagonist, who was also obsessed with chess, were a fictional exaggeration. But they were not. When a subject (in this case, chess) completely preoccupies your life, then it also overruns your dreams. This is how Zweig's hero describes it: "... if I dreamt of people, all they did was move like the bishop or the rook, or hopscotch like the knight."

A decade or so later, when I was living in the Greek countryside surrounded by olive and orange groves, I gradually became an amateur arborist (I didn't even know the word for it before). With local help, I harvested the olives and took them to the nearby oil press to produce my own organic extra virgin olive oil. From December to March, I monitored the citrus trees, tasting mandarins, oranges, and grapefruit to determine when they reached their peak sweetness and were ready to harvest. Then I pruned the trees and fertilized the ground. This was a completely new universe. How could I have lived all my life without knowing its wealth of pleasures and lessons, its surprises and beauty? Still, how could I also have lived without ever knowing of Anderssen's Evergreen chess game or Dr. Irene Pepperberg's African gray parrot Alex, the first animal ever to demonstrate two-way verbal communication with humans and one of the very few animals to show comprehension of abstract ideas?

All these beautiful, endless universes exist in eternal obliviousness to most people, as they used to exist for me. Yet how many more are there that I will never be aware of? How many more universes exist now around me, within just a thousand-meter radius from my house? In the village nearby, the yogurt maker works in his small workshop to produce his delicious yogurt, while the baker wakes up every morning and bakes in a wood-fired oven following a centuries-old tradition. And they both know their tools and enjoy their work as much as Karpov knows his chessboard and loves devising strategic plans.

Living in our own universe is as natural as living itself. As we are not aware of the flow of our blood, we move and act in our own universe in partial or complete ignorance of the parallel universes that exist around us. In a sense, we do not live in the one universe of Newton and Einstein. If the physical universe is the stage, it is nothing without scripts, musicians, and actors. And these are provided, or rather created, by the mind of Man. It is in these "mental worlds," in these rather self-contained parallel universes, that humanity moves and acts, creates and plays. There are countless such universes enveloping our life. And just as there are many different radio frequencies simultaneously present in a room and we may choose to tune to any one of them to listen to a favorite radio program, we can also choose to move to any "universe of Being" we like. These universes are as many as the number of possible human endeavors and activities; so, no one human being can ever dream of entering but a handful of them. We must be grateful when we have become aware of the existence of a few. If we manage to go further and also discover some of the beauties in them, then we have traveled a long way.

But to discover the beauties inherent in some of these other universes, we must truly enter them by going through the life experiences of the members of these universes, even if only for a short period of time. We must at some point strive to become, in the fullness of term, not only a chess player, a parrot lover, or an arborist, but also a musician, a painter, a cook, a potter, a mountaineer, a fisherman. It is by doing this that we deepen our relationship with the world, enrich our life immensely, and strengthen our bonds with our fellow humans residing in other universes. These other universes then cease to mystify us, for we gradually become more aware of their intrinsic qualities, their inner substance and delicate meanings.

Yet, there's also another reason, probably the most important, for why we ought to strive to live for a while in some of the other universes that surround us: *it is by experiencing what it really means to belong to another universe that we come to truly understand our own.* When a chess player immerses himself into the world of birds and ends up loving a parrot as much as his favorite chess game, his universe is not the same again. For it is henceforth experienced through an expanded vision of the world: his love of chess ceases to be singular and obsessive; it becomes one of a variety of loves that extend beyond the chess universe. And when he sees someone passing by, holding his parrot, he can empathically experience the other person's love for his bird by relating it to both his own love of chess and the experience of love he has learned from immersing himself in the world of birds.

To become a conscious being in your own universe, you first have to be enlightened by experiencing the consciousness of others. Only in this way can your own choice in life become a true choice; that is, a true act of conscious volition. Then, by reclaiming—through an act of free will—your already existing life choices in your own universe, you become free of the bonds of heredity and society that placed you there in the first place.

In a sense, we reach Descartes's method from the opposite end: we do not question our beliefs through a negation. We do not begin by throwing off what we have. We try to move outward from where we are, encompassing the living universes that envelop our being and actions. Through a mental expansion, we come to truly understand the little universe we have chosen to inhabit—its uniqueness and beauty, but also its biases and limitations.

Only by learning to love a parrot can one ever truly understand what it means to play chess.

Infinite Microcosms

Infinity is almost always associated with vast entities. We think of the universe as being situated in infinite Space; of Time as extending infinitely along a line backward (the past) and forward (the future); we imagine two parallel straight lines moving forever along a path and somehow meeting (or not meeting!) at infinity; we think of integers repeatedly multiplied by powers of ten as having endlessly increasing zeros. Infinity is grand, overwhelming, inconceivable. And we see ourselves immersed in it as little insignificant ants: humbled, consumed, vanishing.

Yet there is another infinity: the infinity of the small. The infinity inherent in what seems to be finite. This is the infinity of the limitless degrees of magnification with which a microscope can explore what appears contained and measurable. As it turns out, with every new degree of magnification, a microscope discovers new worlds. What was the domain of biology becomes the domain of chemistry, which in turn gives way to the world of physics—CERN's 27-kilometer-long Large Hadron Collider in Geneva is nothing but a giant microscope delving deeper and deeper into the never-ending world of subatomic particles. The more we explore the apparently finite, the more we realize it is boundless. With every new level that is revealed to us, new deeper layers appear below. As it turns out, it is not only infinity that consists of a series of discernable finites, but also the finite. The finite forever eludes and confounds us, just like infinity.

Yet most of us are unaware of this *infinity in the finite*. Or if we are, we do not seem to be overwhelmed by it. The slow unveiling of the infinite in the finite seems like an illusion. For the finite always feels part of our own familiar, graspable, contained world. However, this other infinity ought to puzzle us even more, for unlike the spatial and temporal infinities of astronomy or the abstract infinities of mathematics, it somehow stealthily intrudes into our everyday life. And sometimes it may shudder us to our core.

When I set out to travel around our planet in order to "see" the world, treating it as if it were one huge country, a single destination, I was of the impression that our globe was finite. And that, being finite, it was more or less "knowable" in its most general features—as all finites seem to be. Yet, after a couple of years, and especially after my Indonesian experience, I realized that the world is composed of what I now call *infinite microcosms*. I subsequently came to document that epiphany to Indonesia in *Destination Earth*:

> With 1,000 inhabited islands, this seemingly small corner of the planet turned out to be an immense galaxy unto itself. The accumulated enormity of these islands transcends the limits of our globe. Through their apparent smallness, like grains of sand, they stretch out to reach the infinity of the universe. It now became clear to [me] that our planet, though seemingly finite, is destined to remain forever unknowable and unexplorable. For even if all else is known and traversed, there will always remain the Infinite Microcosm of Indonesia—the fatal battleground of any world-traveler.

The above quote was a rather poetic way of expressing the simple realization that to "see" the islands of Indonesia alone would take my whole life, and to explore the whole world would take many more life-times.

Indonesia actually belongs to what may be called a *geographical* infinite microcosm—a great many islands spread across an archipel-ago. But there are other types of infinite microcosms: There are *natural* ones, such as the infinite varieties of animals, insects, microbes, and plants in the Amazon rainforest. There are *cultural* ones, such as the in-numerable traditions of the Balinese people.

Yet the commonest infinite microcosms are actually the ones near-er to us: our own cities! Large cities are infinite microcosms. And these microcosms are almost invisible, since we are constantly immersed in them. London, for example, with its 200 museums, over 800 attractions of all types, thousands of restaurants, and clubs—and a ceaselessly re-newed stream of plays, concerts, and all sorts of other events—is an *urban* infinite microcosm. The more you explore it, the more you dis-cover that you can never truly know it. Another such microcosm—of a totally different character—is medieval Fez in Morocco. Every alley and every house of Fez contains history and treasures of never-ending diversity. Fez is the magical Arabia of our childhood imagination, and no number of visits could ever exhaust its innumerable gifts.

Both London and Fez are *microcosms*, contained in a small area of the Earth, but they are also *infinite* because their substance is spread over many other dimensions beyond the physical. A city is not just its monuments, parks, gardens, and buildings, but also its history, art, so-ciety, cultural life, the dishes served in its restaurants, the plays in its theaters, the young people conversing and dancing in the clubs. Along each cobbled street of historic Fez and behind each door of central London, there are myriad hidden worlds to be discovered, layers to be uncovered. Even the most curious of Londoners have not yet managed to explore the greater part of their own city.

But the concept of infinite microcosms does not only relate to our efforts to explore and know countries and cities, or the physical and social world in general. Once observed, the concept will be seen to apply to many other aspects of life: Beethoven's music is not finite, for new depths are revealed with every repeated listening to any of his pieces. Not to mention the fact that for each of his compositions, there are hundreds of expert treatises and essays offering endless insights into Beethoven's music and its appreciation. Similarly, Carl Jung's writings are not finite: the insights about the stages of life that lie in them are slowly revealed through repeated readings as we grow up. The inexhaustible depth of Jung's writings may be said to be infinite with respect to our finite ability to both comprehend them and apply them to our everyday life.

The fact that we are surrounded by all sorts of infinite microcosms need not make us feel alienated from what we thought was knowable and contained. On the contrary, this simple realization may open up a new way of looking at the world. Suddenly, we obtain X-ray eyes that see through every finite in our world, transforming it into a possible or a real infinity.

Behind everything we think we already know, behind every experience we've experienced once, behind every place or piece of music or even every familiar object that surrounds us, there are always more layers to be uncovered, more worlds to be discovered, more life to be revealed and enjoyed.

Our Compartmented Mind

The most disconcerting discovery is to find that every part of
us — intellect, will, sense-mind, nervous or desire self, the heart,
the body — has each, as it were, its own complex individuality
and natural formation independent of the rest; it neither agrees
with itself nor with the others nor with the representative ego
which is the shadow cast by some central and centralising self on
our superficial ignorance. We find that we are composed not of
one but many personalities and each has its own demands and
differing nature. Our being is a roughly constituted chaos ...

— Sri Aurobindo, *The Synthesis of Yoga*

❖ ❖ ❖

We all have a compartmented mind.

We manage to hold simultaneously many conflicting ideas by
keeping them in separate compartments in our mind. Our mental
worlds are not, as many of us like to believe, nicely ordered, self-consistent, clean, and settled. But it is not just ideas that we compartmentalize. In addition to beliefs, views, and opinions, we also hold contradictory emotions about people or situations. We even have contradictory

desires. And of course, as a result of all this, many of our actions are contradictory.

A self-proclaimed bird-lover keeps in a different mental compartment the fact that he often eats chicken for dinner. A Christian priest who teaches the sanctity of life has no qualms about blessing weapons or whole armies that kill. A doctor who urges his patients to quit smoking is himself a smoker. Parents punish their kids for not reading books although they never themselves read. Many of us ask for privacy yet post all the details of our lives on social media. Or we accuse others of lying although we lie ourselves.

But we are rarely aware of our internal contradictions. We do not see them, or when we do, we are not truly puzzled by them. On a few rare occasions, we may feel some discomfort at discovering that we hold contradictory views, but we soon find a way to throw our worries under the carpet and do not brood over them.

Psychology has a term for our ability to hold two contradictory views simultaneously: *cognitive dissonance*. Psychologists have performed thousands of experiments over the last seventy years or so to discover how we go about resolving such contradictions and have discovered a few interesting (albeit occasionally quite self-evident) behaviors. For example, they found that if someone makes a public statement that contradicts his long-held views, since he cannot change the public statement, he tends to modify his views, which can be changed, to conform with the stance he took publicly.[5] They also found that a smoker who acknowledges that smoking is bad for his health may use a number of rationalizations to justify his inconsistent behavior: he may claim he is more likely to die in a road accident than from smoking, or that he would rather live a shorter and happier life than a long and deprived one. Psychologists have claimed that such *a posteriori* rationalizations (usually forced upon people by others) are attempts to eliminate the

5   See *A Theory of Cognitive Dissonance* by Leon Festinger (1957).

cognitive dissonance. But I actually think it is the exact opposite: rather than reduce the dissonance, such rationalizations cement it!

Overall, I would argue that psychologists have approached this whole subject backward from the very beginning. In most of their experiments, they have explored how humans go about dealing with their contradictions *after someone else has forced them to confront them.* They have assumed, without any justification, that people feel psychologically uncomfortable when confronted by their contradictions and that this is why they try to resolve them. This assumption dictates that the experiments manufacture situations in which the participants have been forced to face their cognitive dissonances and do something about them. Well, it may not come as a surprise to discover that people may indeed come up with some rationale to explain their contradictions when another person forces them to confront them. But unless others point to these contradictions, most people are rarely aware of the existence of any dissonance in their thought or behavior.

Even when someone is conscious of their inner contradictions, they still do what they please, having developed an answer at the ready for anybody who points out their inconsistent behavior! The smoker *consciously* chooses to maintain two separate mental compartments: holding the fact that smoking is bad, and continuing to smoke. Contrary to what psychologists have assumed, unless he is prompted by others, he will rarely if ever try to spontaneously eradicate or even mitigate these contradictory views and behaviors. We have learned to live with our contradictions from a young age and do not allow them to interfere with our daily life or disturb our psychological well-being. If this were not so, we would observe on a regular basis many people openly struggling with and sharing the internal contradictions that trouble them—we don't. We would also see a good number of them succeeding in their struggle, i.e., managing to live with no or at least with a modicum of contradictions. I have yet to meet such a person!

The reality that we indeed do live with our contradictions, without an inner eye overseeing our internal mental segregations, was first explored by Socrates. In Plato's dialogue "First Alcibiades," Socrates confronts his young pupil Alcibiades who thinks he is fit to become a politician and rule Athens. Through elaborate questioning, Socrates makes Alcibiades initially admit that in order to be a leader, one has to have some special qualities, and then he makes him acknowledge that he lacks those qualities, therefore admitting that his ambition to rule is irrational and unfounded. It is one of the first examples of someone forcing another person to acknowledge his internal contradictions. But we can easily admit that it is not just Alcibiades but all of us who think we can "do better" than those who rule us despite the fact that we have not had any appropriate training for the job or any related experience. Quite tellingly, we know from history that Alcibiades seems not to have learned the lesson of his wise teacher—for he *does* enter politics at a young age and subsequently becomes a menace to Athens. Alcibiades's story augments the argument that *even after* people are confronted with their contradictions, even after they acknowledge them, they have no problem keeping them apart with some simple "smoker-style" rationalization and moving on with their original plans!

Our compartmented mind can most clearly be seen in the way we filter our observations. One of the strongest examples that never ceases to amaze me is the way we view the spring season. Every spring, a profusion of new plants and insects enters our life. All these colors and movements capture our attention and even inspire us. A great number of poems, from Wordsworth's "Daffodils" to Hardy's "Proud Songsters,"[6] praise this dazzling show of colors, sounds, and vitality. But what astonishes me is the almost universal blindness to the fact that all of these entities are short lived: for every cicada that sings, another falls dead from a branch; for every blooming flower, there's one wilting;

---

6   I reproduce this latter poem in its entirety at the opening of "The Uniqueness of Man."

for every colorful fluttering butterfly, there's a dead one on the ground being eaten by ants. Every spring, the whole life cycle of Nature seems to shrink—living things appear for a day or two and then vanish. In no other season is life and death so visibly present and intertwined. But most of us, including sometimes our great poets who usually become more inspired by Life, somehow cut out the death part! We place death in another mental compartment and ignore it. Even when a little moth enters our mouth and we ... eat it by mistake, or a small spider gets caught in our hair and, while trying to liberate it, we kill it, we still compartmentalize our vision to see only life. The words of Vivekananda come to mind here:

> There is no action which does not bear good and evil fruits at the same time. To take the nearest example: I am talking to you, and some of you, perhaps, think I am doing good; and at the same time I am, perhaps, killing thousands of microbes in the atmosphere; I am thus doing evil to something else. When it is very near to us and affects those we know, we say that it is very good action if it affects them in a good manner. For instance, you may call my speaking to you very good, but the microbes will not; the microbes you do not see, but yourselves you do see. The way in which my talk affects you is obvious to you, but how it affects the microbes is not so obvious. ... He who in good action sees that there is something evil in it, and in the midst of evil sees that there is something good in it somewhere, has known the secret of work.

Vivekananda points to what is most probably the biggest of all illusions we live by—that we "do no harm." The majority of us think of ourselves as "being good." Yet every day during our morning walk, we kill a number of living organisms, as the excerpt above describes, without being aware of it. We harm unwittingly not only animals, but also other humans.

We judge our own actions by our intentions, and even when we discover that we have done someone some harm, we still maintain the view that we "are good" since our intentions were good. As it is said: the road to hell is paved with good intentions. Although we judge ourselves by our intentions, others judge us by our deeds. We mentally segregate our intentions from our actions when they are not in harmony because we cannot face the negative outcomes of our actions. *Yet irrespective of how hard we try, we cannot avoid harming others.* Nowhere is this theme better explored than in the ingenious comedy series *Curb Your Enthusiasm*, where the protagonist and creator of the series, Larry David, who basically plays himself, becomes entangled in weird situations in which, despite his often sincere efforts to avoid harming others, he ends up insulting or injuring nearly everyone he encounters. A repeated theme is the conflict between Larry's commitment to being absolutely truthful and his efforts to please others. When he is overly truthful, he hurts people, and when he tells lies to please them, his lies are later exposed and he again unwittingly hurts them! The upshot is that there's no middle way of behaving properly in our complicated society with its many contradictory social norms, nor a way of avoiding conflicts, because one cannot be *both* absolutely truthful and likable.

At the extreme end of "doing no harm" is none other than what our parents, teachers, governments, and churches teach us: "do not kill." Yet these very people and institutions send us to the army to learn how to do the exact opposite. A number of countries, including my own, still have mandatory military service, while all governments retain the right to call all men to arms at will. Murder is prohibited, unless it is sanctioned for a war that others decide is just. We are all, in a sense, potential murderers that may at any moment be called to service! Yet we again compartmentalize this, and when the time to fight comes, we create similar rationalizations to those of the smoker: "we kill in self-defense," or "we kill (*other* families) to protect *our* families," or "we kill for our country/god/beliefs." It seems that our institutions also have a compartmented mind—since they are, after all, a reflection on a grander scale of our own personal nature. They keep in different mental chambers contradictory policies, teachings, and actions. Neither self-consistency nor harmony of words and deeds inform such behavior. It is *expediency* that is the driving force behind the innumerable schizophrenic policies of human society.

Another good example of mental compartmentation between intentions and actions, which is related to another type of "killing," is vegetarianism. Many become vegetarians not in order to simply have healthier eating habits but to avoid killing animals. Vegetarians have arbitrarily placed plants in the category of the nonliving and feel justified eating them even though plants are also living entities. The rationalization is that plants are not sentient, have no feelings, do not suffer, and so on. Yet still, plants are alive. Even if we choose to reject Peter Tompkins and Christopher Bird's case in their controversial *The Secret Life of Plants* (1973), in which the authors ascribe even sentience to plants, we must acknowledge a lot of truth in Peter Wohlleben's recent bestseller *The Hidden Life of Trees*: he has accumulated a lot of evidence that trees become part of communities where the younger trees learn from the older ones, there is communication between them, they express "feelings" such as fear and pain, and they are nearer to the animal kingdom than we have heretofore believed. Vegetarians may not kill one type of living entity, but they still kill another.

The vegetarian denial is part of a larger denial, which is the oldest, most deeply ingrained, and probably the most dazzling example of our compartmented mind: *we are animals but never think of ourselves as such!* Perhaps nothing is more invisible to us in our everyday life than the awareness of our animal nature. We are animals, yet we place this fact in a very remote mental compartment that we rarely visit. We have animal bodies, yet we do not see these bodies because we hide them with clothing. We "kill to eat and rob the newly born of its mother's milk to quench our thirst," as Khalil Gibran eloquently puts it, but we cook our food and cover it with colorful sauces, turn the milk into refined French cheeses, and serve everything on a plate so that we don't look like pigs or hyenas when we eat. We produce excrement, but we use elaborate toilets with seats and flushes that we may dispense with it as fast as possible. And we have turned copulation into "sex"—an activity that we have disassociated from the function of reproduction.

Well, we have a compartmented mind, we are this contradictory species—what do we do about it?

As already suggested, most of us are not interested in resolving our contradictions not just because we rarely see them—or upon seeing them, simply rationalize them in weird ways—but mainly because being contradictory beings is part of our nature. We have a compartmented mind not because of a fault in our makeup but because *this is* our makeup. We have such a mind, and we are inconsistent and imperfect beings, in the same way as our memory is imperfect or as our knees cannot withstand a jump from thirty meters high. Just as we know the limitations of our memory and our knees and adapt our behavior accordingly, knowing the limitations of our ability to be self-consistent and noncontradictory allows us to be less critical of ourselves and especially of others—in whom we can now more easily see a reflection of ourselves. But most importantly, I think that we need to *become aware, observe, and study* our compartmented mind in order to better know ourselves. By regularly reviewing our mental compartments, the inconsistencies between our intentions and actions as well as our contradictory actions, we better understand how we and other people function.

That said, the more philosophical of us, or those who cannot easily rest in peace once they discover their internal contradictions, may wish to go a step further and boldly try to eliminate them. Such an ambitious endeavor is possible, but it must be understood that it can never be completed. For irrespective of how many of our contradictions we eradicate, there will always be many more invisible ones that we will never have access to, as well as a number that we will end up deciding to live with. Absolute self-consistency, harmony of emotions, thoughts, and deeds is something we may keep striving to achieve, but it will always be an unattainable goal.

The Conscious Suffering of Development

When we learn to drive a car, we are anxious, struggle, sometimes even suffer. Most importantly, we are continuously conscious. Learning is a process *in* and *through* consciousness. When learning ends, its final reward is *unconsciousness*: we can drive a car while unconsciously listening to music, looking out the window, talking with our friends. Mechanical action means acquired knowledge. However, it also means the absence of learning! For the process of learning is always conscious and nonmechanical.

Unconsciousness signifies both the consummation and the end of learning.

In a sense, then, the more things we do unconsciously in our lives, the more we operate in the absence of learning. The more we move mechanically and without struggle in our lives, the more we remain outside the process of acquiring new knowledge. Taking this very simple idea to its logical conclusion, we first see that effort, exertion, discipline, diligence, and other such qualities associated with the learning process (which our teachers of old strove to teach us!) signify development, moving ahead. Second and more importantly, we see that at the peak of the struggle, where effort and exertion approach or become suffering and even pain (mental, psychological, or physical), we are also at the peak of acquiring new knowledge or skills. The difficult struggle forces us to somehow "come back to consciousness" and jump out of the automation of everyday life. The athlete, who has already done fifty push-ups and physically suffers to do the final ten in order to reach sixty, knows that it is these last ten that will reap him the greatest benefit. And the student of the German language knows that it is in the painful mastering of the difficult grammar that lies the final conquering of the language.

It is not that the more the pain and suffering, the greater the learning. Rather, the degree of pain and suffering is related to the degree of consciousness we bring to bear upon the process of learning. Just as the athlete must exert the maximum mental and physical concentration to achieve those last ten push-ups and just as the German language student must strive to break his old mental maps to create new grammatical mind-paths, similarly, the profoundest knowledge and the most extraordinary mental or physical skills are acquired through the most conscious experience of struggle, pain, and suffering.

But is this suffering true suffering? The athlete himself chose his sport, his goals, his training method, and his suffering! The language student chose to learn German and then set a target to painfully master it. Real suffering, irrespective of whether it is imposed from without or is generated within, is suffering for which we can find no purpose or aim. Self-chosen suffering, as is the suffering of the masochist, is not true suffering. So anybody suffering in any field of his life, provided that that field was self-chosen, has no right to blame anybody or anything for his seeming difficulties. The conscious suffering of development is not true suffering. Actually, it is a prerequisite for the opposite of suffering: the joy of learning, the joy of mastering new skills, expanding our awareness, moving forward in life.

Here's a test to evaluate where each one of us is at any moment in life with regards to learning and moving forward: How conscious am I of the various activities in my life? How many of these activities, processes, jobs are mechanical and automatic? How much struggle and exertion, but also pain and suffering, do I experience?

Often, I hear people say, "Now I'm settled down and married; I own a house, have a good job and two kids. Why bother learning a new language/reading a history book/obtaining a new skill? I'm done!" Many people voluntarily put a stop to their own development in the name of having fewer problems. Yet, a person seemingly without any problems or struggles in life is a person who does not develop. Such a person may have achieved the calmness of mechanical unconscious living, the security and safety of the known, the peace of inactivity. But do all these amount to "happiness"? Or does this inactivity and apparent peace—a state devoid of struggle and learning—create a sense of meaninglessness that in turn becomes the cause of an inner psychological unsettledness or disturbance that is experienced unconsciously and thus becomes self-defeating? Is the "settled-down" individual above truly happier than the striving, suffering seeker? Or is there deeply within him a permanent vacuum of meaninglessness, not unlike the *seemingly* settled person explored in the second essay of this book, that forbids him from reaping the fruits of his alleged peace of mind? For an unconscious, mechanical living must, by extension, incorporate the unconsciousness of one's own happiness! The peaks of joy, like the peaks of pain, are *conscious* peaks.

Effort, exertion, struggle, pain, and suffering are irrevocably connected with our development. They are also connected with how conscious and nonmechanical we are in our lives. *Loving* the suffering of learning lies at the heart of *living* with it. And living the "unsettled life" of the ever-learning lies at the heart of the best possible settling-down: forever developing.

Suffering as a Dissonant Chord

All problems of existence are essentially problems of harmony.
— Sri Aurobindo, *The Life Divine*

Ingenious notes plugged into a motived score,
These million discords dot the harmonious theme
Of the evolution's huge orchestral dance.
— Sri Aurobindo, *Savitri*

❖ ❖ ❖

Suffering is a dissonant chord.

What is a dissonant chord? It is a musical chord that has the quality of momentarily giving the impression of being out of tune with the rest of the music.

Its role, which is an inherent part of its "nature," is to give a special kind of harmony to the whole, i.e., to ultimately give a consonant effect. Through the tension it creates, the subsequent resolution becomes concordant and pleasant. Its *final* effect is to be a harmonious part of the whole through its momentary seemingly unharmonious quality.

So in what sense then is a dissonant chord "dissonant"? How can it be "out of tune" when it is an indispensable part of the whole structure, the complete composition?

It is dissonant only temporarily, when examined by someone concentrating on a small part of the composition and treating it as an independent entity that exists by itself. But the small part is not independent of the whole. A dissonant note has no function outside the context in which it is placed within a composition. A note by itself can be dissonant in isolation, but notes are meaningless and functionless in isolation. Music is rather a sequence of notes. It unravels as a development in time and its whole structure depends on the harmonious relation of its parts.

This musical analogy may shed light on the problem of suffering: if suffering is a dissonant chord, then only the whole can place suffering in its correct perspective. Our constant preoccupation with our sufferings, with what momentarily seems dissonant and therefore bad, harmful, out of place, is then similar to that of a musically uninitiated person's obsession with examining the dissonance of individual chords of Wagner or Stravinsky in order to figure out why their compositions are great despite the fact that they include so many dissonances. The uninitiated may ask: "Why does *The Rite of Spring* sound so good, why is it such a great piece of music when there are so many ugly notes (and rhythms) in it?" It soon becomes obvious to him that his quest is doomed, for something cannot be defined as ugly or dissonant when it ends up being an integral part of a grander totality that is beautiful and consonant. He realizes that the apparent ugliness of a dissonant chord is an illusion, for its life lasts only for a small interval and its … dissonant effect is canceled as soon as the whole piece comes to a consonant resolution.

Similarly, if we stop searching for an *immediate and direct* explanation of our sufferings and instead try to find the specific role they play within the *whole* composition of our life, and all Life, then we will begin to discover that suffering has a big role to play in our life that is not immediately perceptible. By viewing suffering as a dissonant chord, we become open to the possibility that suffering is not an evil stranger intruding on our life but a potential friend who may reveal his true identity at some later stage.

On one level, we have all those instances when an ordeal leads finally to a favorable outcome. For example, we are fired from our job and feel horrible, only to be offered a much better and more fulfilling job a month later. Or we suffer because a friend or our beloved has betrayed us and left us, only to later on discover that he or she has subsequently committed more heinous acts from which we were spared. These instances exemplify mental and physical trials through which we must go before our personal world can expand.

On a second level, with which we can all relate immediately, we have the suffering inherent in our development and growth on our way to adulthood. We may be punished in school or at home for a misdemeanor we committed. Or we suffer because of friction with our friends. At the time we may feel oppressed by our teachers or parents, or feel depressed by the unfair treatment of our classmates. But later in life, we recognize the benefit of what our teachers did and the value of our struggles to communicate with our friends. Similarly, during late adolescence, men in many societies have to go through hardships to become men, or serve in the military as part of the duty to the fatherland. These hardships, seemingly unnecessary at the time, are later on valued for strengthening character and preparing us to leave the family and create our own home. Most importantly, later as adults we all accept some form of what in the previous essay I referred to as the conscious suffering of development. Every form of personal growth has been associated with some form of struggle or suffering. Effort, exertion, stress, and pain are irrevocably connected with our development. The athlete, the artist, the craftsman, the scientist, the engineer have to struggle to master their respective fields, and the greater the "trials and tribulations," the greater, usually, the mastery achieved.

On a third level, the resolution of the dissonant chord of suffering may also come about in cases of even extreme suffering. In these instances, what usually resolves the suffering is *a new understanding* that transforms the way we see things. An example of one such event involving a quite common occurrence in life is told by Victor Frankl in his magnum opus, *Man's Search for Meaning*. In the book, Frankl describes another doctor who entered his office with severe depression following the loss of his beloved wife two years earlier. Frankl asked him what would have happened if he had instead died before his wife, to which the doctor replied that for his wife this would have been even more terrible to bear.

"You see, doctor," said Frankl, "such a suffering has been spared her, and it was you who have spared her this suffering—to be sure, at the price that now you have to survive and mourn her."

It seems that after this remark, a big weight was lifted from the doctor's suffering soul, for as Frankl so eloquently writes in what is a recurrent theme in his book, "suffering ceases to be suffering at the moment it finds meaning, such as the meaning of a sacrifice." By helping the doctor see his state from a new vantage point—that of the *totality* of his life, rather than from the narrow perspective of his current personal suffering—the doctor understood that what seemed meaningless and hence dissonant in isolation turned out to have had a deeper meaning and harmony in his life as a whole: *his suffering was the suffering his wife was being spared of!* Unless they die simultaneously in an accident, this is the fate of *every* person who outlives his or her spouse. When viewed from Frankl's perspective, every dissonant chord of suffering of every elderly person who has lost a beloved can be likewise resolved via a similar new understanding that harmonizes it with the totality of life (and death) of *both* oneself and one's spouse.

But what happens when the suffering is not only extreme, but there is no evidence or any possibility for anything in the universe bringing about any future resolution? How can any good possibly ever come out of, say, physical incarceration or a permanent handicap? Suddenly, we realize that such suffering cannot be resolved by some later event, nor by a subsequent reaping of the fruit of personal growth, nor by any new understanding—possibilities we've already examined. In other words, what happens when Nature does not itself provide either the resolution or hints that such a resolution exists? Well, if we stick to the view that suffering is a dissonant chord, we may see this lack of any provided resolution as a challenge to *create* the resolution ourselves!

Rather than passively waiting for Life itself to provide the harmonizing notes, we create them.

The dissonant chord of suffering can then be considered as "a given chord" that Life asks us to subsequently harmonize willfully through our own actions. So our suffering ceases to be a one-of-a-kind static entity and becomes *a dynamic potentiality* whose final true nature and meaning in our life and Life in general is dependent upon us. By struggling to incorporate the dissonant chord of suffering into the totality of our life, in effect we become *the composers* of a new life in which this chord ceases to be disharmonious.

Having been imprisoned in a concentration camp, Victor Frankl chose to transmute his suffering into something beautiful, consonant, harmonious—a philosophy of meaning. In addition to founding a new school of psychotherapy, logotherapy, he wrote one of the greatest books of the twentieth century. When Beethoven started to lose his hearing in his early twenties, he eventually triumphed over it by using it as the oil that fired his inspiration and creativity. The music Beethoven could not hear with his ears became the music he struggled to hear in his mind, and the music which would in great part end up expressing none other than this very struggle. His Fifth Symphony, which was posthumously named "Fate," is therefore a supreme transmutation of the dissonant chord of suffering (his deafness) into a beautiful harmonious symphonic work. In this unique and rare case of Beethoven, we see suffering leading to a double harmony: he harmonized his life's suffering by subsequent work and action that transcended it, and he created great "harmonious" music that expressed this same work in the medium of musical language itself! This symphony is the perfect example of how our work can transform ourselves, our life, and all Life into something beautiful and even glorious. The greatest dissonant chord in Beethoven's life, his extreme adversity, became in the end the catalyst for a unique triumph that led to his becoming one of the greatest men in history.

But of course, the pinnacle of all life-examples of resolving the dissonant chord of suffering is none other than the West's most important figure, Jesus, whose Passion became *the condition* for his glory. The final "composition" of Jesus's exemplary and inspiring life lies in the extreme dissonance of an unspeakable Passion becoming the epitome of harmony through the extreme act of love and forgiveness for his tormentors—an act that gave the suffering a higher meaning. It is the resultant harmonious sequence and blending of the two opposing chords that led to the supreme consummation and glory of Jesus's life. Contemporary examples of people who have managed to convert their extreme adversity and suffering into a great life *by virtue of their adversity* include Martin Luther King, Nelson Mandela, and the Dalai Lama.

Viewing even extreme suffering as a dissonant chord rather than as some anomaly in an impersonal universe helps us discover ways to transmute it into a newly created *personal universe* in which the dissonance is resolved by and through our own actions. Just as we do with our handling of the matter and energy of the cosmos, channeling it into the myriad forms of everything we create as mankind, we may transform our sufferings, the dissonant chords of our life, into something consonant, thereby creating a unique composition of a creative life that has never before appeared in the universe.

By transposing "the problem of suffering" into "a problem of harmony," it ceases to be a dark mystery, a meaningless cruelty, an inexplicable intrusion upon the Creation. The problem of suffering then ends up becoming none other than the way it harmonizes with the rest of our life, albeit having initially seemed out of place and dissonant. Suffering then may be viewed as simply one element of the overall harmony of the cosmos—a harmony that may be experienced by us humans in particular as furthering our development and helping us expand our World. Taking the analogy of the dissonant chord to its culmination, we need only take one further step that will allow us to accept the non-negative function of suffering in our life, and in some sense even explain it rationally to ourselves in a satisfactory manner.

We can consider suffering to be not only an indispensable part of the Becoming's own process, but a *constituent element* of the Becoming's overall harmonious composition.

The Visible and the Invisible Worlds

I admire a big tree full of red pomegranates—hanging like Christmas tree balls. I know that just below it there's another "subterranean tree" that sustains it. Less impressive to the human eye, colorless, invisible—the roots

I sit on a bench on a busy street and observe the passersby. I don't focus on their clothes nor try to imagine their naked bodies. With X-ray vision, I see their hearts pumping blood, their lungs inhaling air, their kidneys filtering internal juices. I don't see lean human bodies, but bones and sinew and blood.

I look at the moon and stars. I think of how they remain in their orbits. I suddenly see in my mind's eye Newton's and Einstein's laws—numbers and symbols and equations.

I listen to a Bach concerto. I stop following the music and dissect the process: there are sheets of music and violin strings and metal wind tubes and sound waves moving through the air and an eardrum that translates all this into music.

I read a poem. It talks about objects and people and situations of this world. But it transports me to another world where these things obtain another meaning and create another world—the same world that gave rise to the poem. An invisible world.

Everything we see, every natural or man-made object, every natural phenomenon, every animal and human activity, every event in the universe has an invisible substratum that sustains it. A substratum that nourishes, guides, informs, determines its form. This invisible entity is vast, and often much vaster than the visible elements it springs forth.

The tree roots sustain the tree above. The internal organs sustain the fleshy body. The physical forces governed by mathematical laws sustain the galaxies. The abstract relations of harmony sustain our art and music. Every higher human activity—our philosophy, psychology, poetry, and art, the principles of our ethics and human conduct—is sustained by our mind.

Wherever we look, whatever we explore, we discover one universal truth: *Everything visible is sustained by something invisible.*

Yet we are the only creatures who have the ability to somehow discover and "see" these invisible worlds. We need only dig a few inches below the ground to discover the tree's vast roots. We need only dissect or use sensors to see our own heart and lungs. We need only study carefully the visible motion of planets and stars to discover the equations that govern their motions. And even if we can never truly "see" with our eyes the laws of physics, harmony, or thought, we may still come to know of their existence in some indirect way.

It is because we discover and finally "see" much of what is hidden that many deny the very existence of the invisible world. If we can dig, dissect, explore our world and ourselves to find what is hidden, they say, then whatever we discover ceases to be part of the invisible. The invisible is not *truly* invisible. It is simply that part of the visible that for some reason or other was not visible to us because of our limited capacity or obstructed vision. The "invisible world," they claim, is only so in as much and for as long as we fail to see it.

Such an assertion may at first seem quite simple and rational. Yet upon closer analysis it is incorrect. For even after these invisible worlds in all the aforementioned fields become discovered, explored, and known, *they still remain* part of the invisible: the tree roots studied by specialized botanists are still *the invisible to us* part of the tree. Our internal organs, even after the doctors cut us open and study them, function without us seeing them or being aware of them, and without us knowing how they do so. The overwhelming majority of people will leave this world without ever having seen their pancreas or liver, and without ever having known how all of our inner parts coordinate harmoniously to sustain our body. Furthermore, it is not just that the tree roots are invisible to us *because* they are below the earth, or that our internal organs are unseen *because* they are covered by our skin. *They are invisible because they were meant to be invisible!* The tree roots that sustain the tree that creates blossoms and fruit, and our organs that sustain our body, which creates buildings and machines and ideas, *must be* invisible in order to properly bring forth their visible elements and perform their functions.

This simple truth becomes even more clear when we examine the most invisible entities of all, the strange entities it took thousands of years of human civilization to discover: the laws of nature. The mathematical laws of physics that rule the cosmos do not pop up *in* the visible universe. These too *were meant* to be invisible. Each time an apple falls on the ground, we do not see next to it Newton's law of gravity hovering in space; each time a supernova explodes, we don't see Einstein's field equations flashing about in that corner of the universe!

Behind the movements of every visible object, animate or inanimate, there are invisible physical laws of motion and thermodynamics, chemical laws of reactions and interactions, biological laws of reproduction and evolution, mental laws of mathematics, logic, reasoning. Yet these laws, which our investigative spirit has discovered, are not part of the visible world—they exist in some domain other than the visible. The invisible could never sustain the visible if it were not of a different substance and quality than the latter and if it did not inhabit another sphere of being and function in a different way. It is exactly because these invisible laws direct and govern all movements without themselves being part of them, i.e., without themselves *residing within* the visible, that they sustain the latter. It is the invisibility of these laws that makes them effective.

Because we never think of the tree roots when we enjoy the cherry blossoms, nor think of our beloved's spleen when we embrace her, nor of the law of gravity every time we trip and fall, we may go about our daily lives remaining in complete ignorance of the invisible world. We accept the reality of the invisible world a hundred times a day, we converse with it, we occasionally study and explore it, but we rarely if ever become aware of its huge importance and the role it plays in our life. Yet, its reality is a fact, hidden though it is in plain sight.

We could divide the invisible world, or rather worlds, because there are many, into two broad categories: the physical or material (that "reside," so to speak, in the observable world and are made of matter), and the ones that exist in our consciousness. The tree roots and our internal organs belong to the first category. The mental, emotional, psychological, and spiritual invisibles belong to the second: our ideas that create our ethics, belief systems, and philosophies; the formulas of harmony and balance that inform our arts; our emotions, which guide our actions; the unconscious workings that lie behind our motives—all are part of our nonmaterial make up. They may have visible effects in the physical world, yet they do not reside *in* the latter. For example, our Will expresses itself in willful acts, but it is invisible, and its nature, even after 5,000 years of philosophical and scientific explorations, still remains uncharted and mysterious.

As for the other invisible world, that of the laws of nature, there have been many philosophical discussions as to whether they reside in the mental or physical world. Maybe they *do* reside in both, since once we formulate these laws mentally/mathematically, we can then use them to predict the motion and interaction of matter—be it the orbits of planets, the functioning of motor engines, or the weather. If the laws of nature were only mental, they would never have had any correspondence with our material world. Still, if it were not for man to discover them in his consciousness, there would never have appeared in the universe buildings and engines, music and art, computers and spaceships.

We need not go further into such philosophical discussions. It is sufficient to acknowledge that in both the physical and the mental worlds we have never ceased to discover more invisible ones. Both the visible and invisible worlds are vast and still uncharted. Just as we keep on discovering new insects and plants, subatomic particles and stars, we also keep discovering new invisible laws of physics and biology, and new abstract ideas that expand our understanding of the world and ourselves.

It is in this latter field, which we may roughly call the field of consciousness, that the greatest breakthroughs are now happening. Up until the end of the nineteenth century, we didn't even know of the existence of the unconscious. Even after a century and a half of psychoanalytical exploration, this vast invisible world has barely been charted. Similarly, the superconscious, that part which lies not below but above consciousness, and which was first studied in ancient times by Hindu and Buddhist mystics and philosophers, is only now being explored systematically. The first major explorations began only a century ago by Sri Aurobindo, who gave us a glimpse of this new and vast territory. According to him, there are five higher levels above our ordinary consciousness: Higher Mind, Illumined Mind, Intuitive Mind, Overmind, and Supermind. This is just a small glimpse into the vast field of strange new invisibles waiting to be discovered and explored.

We must also be open to the possibility of the existence of completely new invisible worlds and phenomena that partake of both the material and mental worlds. There is now overwhelming evidence that such phenomena, studied foremostly by parapsychologists, do actually exist. When the field of parapsychology (hopefully) soon becomes a respected scientific-philosophical discipline and tens of thousands of re-searchers become devoted to its study, new fascinating worlds will be revealed, which will help advance our human civilization to new levels.

And I'm certain that once we enter this new path of exploration, we may be able to tackle, in a more systematic and methodical way, the greatest of all mysteries: for if the general law is that everything visible is sustained by something invisible, is it a big step to assume that the totality of all existence must also obey this ubiquitous internal law of itself? And that behind the whole of the visible universe, there lies an invisible substratum that sustains it?

We may then one day be able to proclaim with a final definitive as-surance that verily:

An Invisible world sustains the Visible.

On Our Connection
with Others

Overlapping Circles

Each one of us is a circle.

In this circle we collect and enclose, as if they were little pebbles, all of our loves, interests, aims, dreams, preoccupations.

We are an amalgam of many elements put together as a result of random events, choices, and coincidences that make up our personal histories. And because of the way we are and the interests we have, we choose to seek interactions with people with whom we have something in common. We pursue acquaintances, build relationships, form friendships, and, most importantly, we *communicate* with others by finding a common ground, or rather *a common area*: we seek out people who have the same or similar pebbles in their circle, and intersect with their worlds by meeting them in these common areas we share.

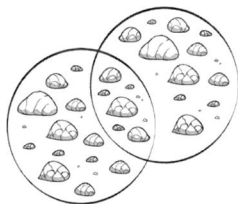

Our communication with others may therefore be likened to that of "overlapping circles." In the shaded area common to both circles—which, incidentally, is called "a union" in mathematics—we communicate with other people and start forming a union. However, although these common interests are the areas where we meet, they also delineate *the limits* of our communication. With the friend who shares an interest in politics, we may not share an interest in literature. With the company of the friends we meet to watch football, we may not go to the theater.

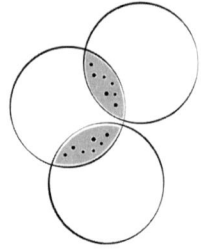

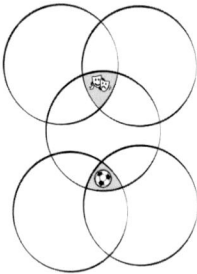

Our circle only partially overlaps with the circles of most others, since each person on earth has a unique set of pebbles, a one-of-a-kind circle. Even with those close friends and family members with whom we have bonds that span decades, our common shaded area is not as extended as we may think. Furthermore, our communication evolves and changes as we grow older, since each one is adding different pebbles to their circles.

There are many who divide people into categories based on the sets of pebbles they can relate to. Some are even high-nosed and picky, always choosing to associate with people from their same professional group or with people with whom they share hobbies. Others place emphasis on historical connections by choosing to associate their entire lives with the same old friends they had in high school, never seeking to expand their circle. Others choose to communicate and form bonds only with people of their same social class, or nationality, or even age. Such approaches to our communicating and bonding with others are based on a hidden yet utterly false assumption: that such associations are "normal" and "natural." But the fact that they are easy and effortless, because they are presented to us by default, or because we simply imitate what everybody else is doing, does not make them any more normal or natural than any other bonds we choose to make. Actually, such a stance is very limiting and impoverishes our social as well as our personal life. By associating only with those who share common interests, we stick to our small set of pebbles, never enlarging our world, and never increasing the number of points at which we touch Life. In the essay "Parallel Universes," I show how our life can be infinitely expanded the moment we depart from our own universe to meet other new universes of activity in which many other people live—universes that lie completely outside our own world, circle, and familiar set of pebbles.

But how are we to form relationships with people when we seemingly have nothing in common? Well, the simple answer is that there are no people with whom we have nothing in common! Actually, there are no living *nor nonliving* objects in the universe with which we have absolutely nothing in common. With all inanimate objects, we share the same atoms and molecules and we obey the same laws of physics (when we touch the fire, we burn like the burning coal in the fireplace, and when we misstep while walking down the stairs … we roll like a stone!). With plants and animals, we share basic sensations; we are all born, we grow, reproduce, die. With other mammals, we share advanced sensations such as sights and sounds, as well as perceptions: animals have models of the world in their minds, as we do, not to mention they too experience love, anger, jealousy, boredom, excitement, and have social lives—as all pet owners know. Most importantly, as I will discuss in a later essay,[7] we all share our existence at the tip of time's arrow.

This simple realization makes us *more open* to approaching others whose circles of interests and loves seem distant from our own. For we know beforehand that there must exist common shaded areas that are to be soon discovered if we have an open mind and an attitude of exploration. There are no boring people. Nor people who "are not for us." They are only boring if *we* are boring! For we have boringly decided to consider our own interests and loves, our own limited set of pebbles, as

---

7   See p. 142.

the measure of what is interesting, important, valuable, and worthy of attention. Whenever we fail to find a common area of communication with another, let us think that the other may also think we are boring, for he too can see nothing in us of interest to *him*.

Even when we meet somebody from another culture with whom we apparently have absolutely nothing in common, if we are open to his world, we will soon start discovering many common pebbles: his basic biological needs are the same as ours—he too eats, rests, sleeps, and snores; he too loves and laughs and sheds tears; he too is curious about life and the world; he too understands the concepts of kindness, hospitality, and friendship. Through these basic overlaps, we may begin communicating on a simple level and then start discovering even more common pebbles. Soon we will see that the number of common pebbles, and consequently the common shaded area of our overlapping circles, increases as we discover parts of the other person's world and integrate them into our own. While we are deepening our communication and union with the other person, we are simultaneously expanding our circle—our world—by including more pebbles in it. Actually, our world expands the more we stop considering our unique set of pebbles to be the measure of all things!

But the shaded areas and the common pebbles we share with others are not the whole story of our communication and bonding with people. The shaded areas show the extent of our communication, not necessarily the depth. For this is not to be found on the edge of the circle, but rather, like in all circles, or rather in all psychological mandalas, it is to be found in the center. Our communication and relationships with others begin to form on the outer rim of common interests, but they always have the potentiality to move towards the center of our being. For within each small field we share with another, there lie deeper truths that reveal the heart and soul of both the other and ourselves. This is so because from the center of the circle, which we may consider to be the soul of our being, emanates the substance of what and who we are. Although we all enclose a unique collection of pebbles, each of these pebbles connects to our center because it is our center that has chosen and formed the collection in the first place.

There is something of the center of a person in each common pebble, in each shared area of our overlapping circles.

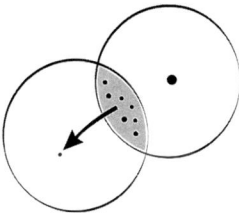

Therefore, we may consider each shared area to be a stepping stone (… composed of many pebbles!) that has the potential to lead us to the other's center. Through the common love we share with someone for jazz, we may end up gradually experiencing love for one another at the deepest level. Through the common interest in modern art we share with a friend, we may end up taking art lessons together, then start reading books together and discussing philosophy, and finally converge towards a common understanding of our life's meaning in the universe. Such movements indicate a motion from the periphery of communication and interaction towards the center. In the end, this leads to an *identity* of the two circles. We then find ourselves not simply sharing parts of our world with the other, but *becoming one* with him. The two separate centers become one, even though they still remain the center of two distinct circles with distinct sets of pebbles.

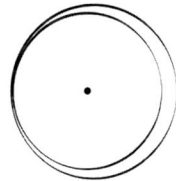

The analogy of the circle and all the subsequent schematics used here offer, as always, a model that helps illuminate various ideas, but this model is not exhaustive, nor, of course, conclusive. For example, there still remains the mystery of how we may experience an identity with another, how we may become one with him at our very center while simultaneously remaining the center of our own circle, which encloses a different world from his. Yet we have all experienced such moments in our life—moments where all differences with the other seem to vanish at the heart and center of our being. We know this is possible, even if we cannot fully comprehend it. We may illuminate all of the above with an example:

In one of the greatest movies of this century, *Little Miss Sunshine*, we see how a group of six completely different characters, who share almost nothing in common apart from being family members, gradually come closer to one another during the span of a small journey in a van. Through basic challenges, such as having to coordinate pushing their ailing van to start the engine, to more complex situations, such as dealing with ambition, betrayal, grief, and more, we see a continual expansion of each person's world, a subsequent deepening of their communication, and an increase of the areas of their overlapping circles. Throughout the movie, we also feel that the family's common love for its little daughter Olive forms the background, or rather the center around which they all move. In the final scene, where, through a creative spontaneous act, all the protagonists join Olive on the dance floor, we basically experience the move from all previous activities on the edge of their overlapping circles towards a center they all suddenly discover they share. The ambitious father, the neurotic mother, the problematic teenager, the homosexual academic—all jump on the dance floor to accompany Olive to the tune of a sex-laden song that was chosen by Olive's now-deceased grandpa to teach her to dance. The ever-increasing number of common elements they all slowly discover they share with one another leads to a deepening of their relationship and to a final movement from the fringes of their circles towards the center. All characters finally become one entity by meeting one another at the heart of their being.

Such character development is not the exclusive domain of movies. We too may seek to both develop and expand our relationships with others through communication, irrespective of how we initially evaluate the prospects of a future bonding with them. And we can do this by being continually mindful of the processes by which we create our bonds and friendships, as well as by meditating on the limited and limiting way we view what we call our "common interests" with others. For each person we meet is a unique circle with a wealth of pebbles and areas of potential commonality that we could never have imagined at the outset.

Love Is as Love Does

"Love is not a feeling. Love is as love does."
— M. Scott Peck, *The Road Less Traveled*

Enough with *words* of love!

Enough with expressions of *feelings* of love!

Enough with romanticized and transient *fallings* in love!

Let's stop the falling!

Love is not words. It is not feelings. It is not becoming obsessed with an *object* of love.

Love is as love does.

Love is *action*. It is conscious striving for the beloved. It is willful thoughtfulness properly planned and executed.

Love is what is expressed in acts of love. It is volitional, not emotional. He or she who loves is engaged in *works of love*.

When you love somebody, ask yourself, "What *acts* of love have I done for him?" When somebody tells you he loves you, try to see beyond his words: Are there any acts in the foreground—or even in the background?

Love is not a feeling that sits; it is a force that acts.

Words of love, feelings of love, and fallings in love are not necessarily bad or empty, *provided* they are followed by relevant action.

There are feelings that stand alone and need nothing beyond themselves to establish their reality: the feeling of awe or fear, the feeling of accomplishment, of restful contentment, of artistic or spiritual contemplation. Yet love belongs to another category of entities that are not quite stand-alone feelings. Just as "feeling daring" may result in acts of bravery, loving is irrevocably connected to the visible expression of loving acts. Stand-alone "feelings of love" are as meaningless as the courage of a supposedly brave man who simply talks about the brave deeds he intends to do, but never does! Love, just as bravery, is not static. "Loving" is not even a "state of being," like, say, sleeping or thinking. It is a "state of doing," such as working in your office, or on the construction site, or fetching the wood for the fireplace. Consequently, loving is identical to love's self-expression in real life. *Loving is not an invisible entity.* It is not ethereal, up there in the sky, nor hidden somewhere deep in our emotional world, nor sitting idly in some poet's mind. Rather, it can be *seen* in the outside world via the actions that emanate from it; it is revealed through the words and movements and actions of our body or mind that express our loving soul. And it becomes a poem of love only after the poet becomes engaged in loving acts, not before. And of course the writing of the love poem, the very *act* of writing it, is yet another act of love.

Furthermore, since loving is an act dependent on our *own actions*, it is independent of other people's actions—including those of the beloved. In this sense, and unlike what common wisdom holds true, love is one-directional and need not even be reciprocated. One of the best expressions of this relinquishing of the need for reciprocation was given 2,000 years ago by Seneca in one of his letters to Lucilius in which he speaks about friendship:

> The wise man, I say, self-sufficient though he be, nevertheless desires friends if only for the purpose of practicing friendship, in order that his noble qualities may not lie dormant. Not, however, for the purpose mentioned by Epicurus ... "That there may be someone to sit by him when he is ill, to help him when he is in prison or in want"; but that he may have someone by whose sickbed he himself may sit, someone a prisoner in hostile hands whom he himself may set free.

In other words, we do not need a friend in order for him to do things for us, but so that *we may have the opportunity to do something for him.* We "need" him so that we may act *for* him. This type of "need" springs from our inner being outward and becomes loving work. This loving service is simultaneously a way of practicing our own already cultivated noble qualities, which will atrophy if they "lie dormant." Paradoxically, as Seneca so ingeniously put it, by practicing friendship we do not only do good to our friends, but to ourselves!

In recent times, the psychiatrist M. Scott Peck distinguished between cathexis and love, or rather the "emotion of love" that is often misunderstood as love itself. Cathexis, put simply, is attraction with dependency: we cathect somebody (or something) when we want to own him or her, when we want to "get something from the person," or even when we need the other person to nurture our own development with little or no regard for the other person's well-being. Cathexis (by which he also classifies the state of "falling in love") is needy and self-centered, and should not be confused with real love.

The concept of love as action directed towards the beloved without any thought of reciprocation and without any feelings of attachment or dependency is actually identical to the ideal of karma yoga, in which work is done for work's sake and not for the rewards it may entail. Through this Eastern ideal of work, we may expand the concept of "love-as-action" to encompass not just love for other people but for the whole animal kingdom and also for inanimate objects or even ideas: we love animals when we *do* something for them (or at least leave them on their own without exploiting them); we love our plants and garden when we take good care of them, when we *serve* them; and, of course, we love our car, our art collection, our ideas when we work to maintain or enrich or defend them, respectively.

And just as the quality of every work is proportional to the passion with which it is done, *the quality of love is related to the passion with which love generates acts of love.* Going a step further, we may identify the quality of love with the quality of the loving work: just as good work requires diligence, discipline, and thoughtfulness, "good love" is the product of wise action, not of blind instinct. As one needs to spend time and energy to learn one's work or to master one's craft, similarly, one must take up the responsibility of love by *learning to love.* And the first step towards this education is to unlearn the false and ubiquitously held notion that love is a feeling or something that resides invisibly outside this world.

But how do we learn to love?

Well, the analogy of mastering a craft continues to serve us well here: just as we become better at our craft by practicing it, *we become better at love by practicing acts of love.* When we meditate on the subject, we will discover that our very first understanding of love—which is also probably the deepest—was obtained through observing and experiencing our parents' loving acts *towards* us. Consequently, our first acts of love were the ones in which we strove to emulate our parents' loving behavior. Through imitation, we cultivated our skill, our ability, our power to love *through* and *by* our loving acts. The extent to which our practice has been continuing ever since is the measure of our current and future ability to love through action.

Some may be offended when they hear that loving can be taught or that love requires conscious effort, discipline, and more in order to be worthy of the name. After all, is not parental love instinctive, is not romantic love spontaneous, is not spiritual contemplation or love towards the Divine something that flows (or ought to flow) effortlessly from our own being irrespective of whether we do anything? Well, actually, when examined carefully, none of these are so: parental love becomes beneficial love only when it is thoughtful and guided by wise decisions, not when it is purely "instinctive"; romantic love may or may not become true love only after the initial honeymoon phase of spontaneous cathexis subsides; and spiritual contemplation, rather than being idle, to quote Brother David Steindl-Rast, is "contemplation in action," which he defines as "a way of coming to know God's love from within by acting it out," or as "that contemplation in which we realize God by acting in love." Real love is conscious, thoughtful, and guided by the human will.

Because love is work, and therefore identical to conscious loving deeds, we may use what we know of the nature of work to shed light on one final aspect of love-as-work that is often misunderstood: self-sacrifice. The highest expression of *any* work is some form of self-sacrifice (in its more ordinary and everyday meaning). In our job, self-sacrifice, whenever it happens, is identical to absolute self-forgetfulness—we "sacrifice" our sense of self when we completely merge, so to speak, with our work, existing only *in* the work we do. As parents, we sacrifice our time, energy, money, and more for the benefit of our children. In friendship, we immerse ourselves in our friends' worlds and are ready to sacrifice whatever we deem necessary in order to be of service to them. In its more extreme and rarer expression, self-sacrifice may mean literally giving one's own life for the beloved. Thus we have Socrates gladly welcoming death in order to both defend his highest ideals and give history's most perfect example of ethical conduct to his beloved students, and Jesus suffering and being crucified for the sake of his beloved humanity, thereby becoming the very embodiment, the paragon of the teaching *Love is Action.*

Although neither self-sacrifice nor suffering need be an integral part of loving action, still, it is by being prepared to gladly sacrifice one's well-being, comforts, wealth, and peace of mind—and, if necessary, to welcome suffering too—that one may be said to have embarked on the Path of Love: a path that has nothing to do with feelings and everything to do with deeds.

"But Everybody Does It!"

It is supposed to be the phrase that vanquishes all opposition: "But *everybody* does it!"

Or its corollary: "But *nobody* does it!"

Your elaborate argument, your opinion and carefully expressed points, amount to nothing. Whatever you have just said or are about to say has already been rejected by an invisible referendum: the overpowering ballot of the masses! The majority, or rather "the multitude" of Seneca, sets the rules of conformity that all must obey. There is no room for errant ideas, opinions, actions, or behaviors.

In the majority of discussions concerning human behavior, the "everybody argument," in one of its many forms, is bound to appear at some point with its almighty force:

   – Why do you do this strange thing?
     – But everybody does it!
   – This is very slow and inefficient.
     – Nobody ever complained before!
   – I would like to request …
     – Nobody has ever requested that!

There is a feeling of security in knowing that we are not alone. Any lack of originality is more than offset by the comfort of knowing we belong to a larger group that behaves similarly. There is also the self-assurance that we cannot be in the wrong. If everybody does it, it *must* be right. The multitude defines social propriety, delineates the right path, declares its exclusive access to the truth.

Without realizing it, we find ourselves simply reacting to the common polls. *All personal action becomes reaction*—similar to the reaction of a politician who feels he did something wrong if his poll ratings have fallen. He tries to modify his behavior to get the polls up again. Yet an unpopular action need not be "wrong" just because the majority thinks so at the time. That's why the good ruler does not try to modify his actions so that they are constantly popular. He knows that months later, after his initial action has been shown to be wise, the majority will gradually end up supporting it. For just like the weather, popular opinion is precarious, shifting, impossible to ever determine with certainty.

Hans Christian Andersen's famous tale "The Emperor's New Clothes" is the perfect criticism of aligning one's actions with what "everybody does." Andersen's story shows that social conformity is in harmony neither with the truth nor reality. On the contrary, although the force of the multitude seems almighty, it is actually *very weak*—the simplest utterance of a child may easily demolish it!

But why does social conformity creep up on us so naturally? Because it is easy. In order to detach from the group, it is necessary to struggle. To use terms from physics: the social gravity is strong, and the force necessary to achieve the escape velocity that would propel one from society to the freedom and weightlessness of outer space must be strong enough to match it. Most are not willing to put in the necessary effort for such a takeoff. Standing on the Earth, feeling the gravity under our feet, is easy, comforting, effortless.

But it is not just the difficulty of the struggle that lies at the heart of the willingness to go along with the force of society's gravitational pull. There is a much stronger and quite invisible force that paralyzes: *fear*.

Fear that our knowledge, ability, talent are lacking. Self-doubt creeps in because we have been conditioned to give unwarranted respect to the common norms: "Who am I to do it differently? The majority knows better." And on the uppermost pedestal stands the greatest fear of them all: *the fear of failure.* A fear that stems from feeling the others' gaze upon us. For the concept of failure exists only *in* society, since all evaluations and judgments pertaining to our actions are defined by society.

Take a Robinson Crusoe living alone on an island. As there is no one there to judge him, his actions are neutral. An action that leads nowhere is simply a dead end for him, not a "failure." Crusoe need only retrace his steps to get it right, or he may try again, or he can simply decide to … sit down and rest. Every action on a remote island is just the natural consequence of the previous action. Likewise, our life is constant struggle without any innate adjectives attached to any effort we make. Our dead ends teach us to identify roads forward when they arise. We only experience reaching a dead end as "failure" because we unconsciously adopt this social characterization of the act as the *reality* of the act. It is the fear of a possible future "failure," discernible primarily in the judgmental gaze of others, that keeps so many from *forming their own ideas or forging their own path.*

Doing what everybody does destroys what everybody *could* have done had each one followed freely his own way. The "everybody does it" stance in life is one of the most significant factors behind modern man's alienation. When we continually align our behavior, wishes, or ideas to those of the multitude, we distort them and end up living a life that is disconnected from our inner being.

What is most disturbing is that this stance also goes against human rationality itself: what everybody does may simply be unwise. And that which nobody has done may be due to a lack of imagination—the time has come for *somebody* to do it! Which brings us to the heart of the matter: each one of us is *somebody.* We are neither "everybody" nor "nobody."

I recall an incident with a New Zealand hotel owner to whom I complained about the fact that the room he had checked me into the previous evening was, contrary to his assurances, very noisy, and I did not sleep all night. His reply was: "Nobody has complained." At that moment, imitating Odysseus in another context,[8] I spontaneously replied: "Well then, I guess my name is Nobody!" I had thereby completely changed the meaning of what he had said, and forced it to conform to reality: the "nobody has complained" (meaning that no other person had yet complained) was transformed into "Mr. Nobody *has just* complained." I could not be dismissed, for there I was, disproving the *no*-body argument by being *some*-body complaining in front of his very eyes.

Whenever anybody tells you about nobody ever having done something, you need only take a similar stance, and become Odysseus: *become the Nobody about to do it!* And when people say "But everybody who listened to the Sirens' song was destroyed," you may reply: "Everybody *else* was destroyed, but I'm Odysseus, and I will bind myself to a mast, listen to the Sirens' enchanting song, and not be destroyed."[9]

The multitude may rule the world, but it doesn't have to rule *you*.

---

8 When asked by the one-eyed giant Polyphemus to tell him his name, the cunning Odysseus replied, "My name is Nobody." When, later in the story, Polyphemus was blinded by Odysseus, who in the meantime managed to escape, he asked for help from his fellow giants. But when they asked him who had blinded him and he said "Nobody," they thought he had become crazy. It is implied that Odysseus had foreseen the whole series of events that would follow his escape.

9 Reference to the Sirens story, again from the *Odyssey*.

There Is Nothing to Understand

We are blinded by name and form. We are hooked on an understanding of the world and other people that is limited by our narrow definitions.

We are appalled by the brutality of those who show no ethical constraints whatsoever, like serial killers. "How could he?" is the common phrase that causes many a sleepless night. This inability "to understand" other people's horrendous acts or crimes is a cause of great pain in our lives. We are baffled and keep trying to understand why some people do what they do. But is such understanding possible?

The serial killer baffles and disturbs us because we have already classified him in the category of "humans." His behavior is outside the human norm and makes no sense to us. But the world is full of *living beings* of myriad forms and behaviors. Just because we name, classify, and place them in a group does not mean that we exhaust their infinite variations. Most importantly, naming is not understanding. On the contrary, *it is the naming that is at the root of all of our confusion.*

If we were to place the serial killer into another category, another class of beings, the "mystery" would suddenly dissolve. Do we ever speak of a lion as being a serial killer? Because a lion, alongside every carnivore in nature, is just that. We too kill millions of other animals for our food. We simply consider that normal, for we have a "good explanation"—we call it "sustenance." It may not help to go so far as to consider as equal the killing of animals for food and the serial killer's obsessive pursuit of his passions and degenerate cravings—even though, from the point of view of the cows and chickens we consume, it is exactly the same. Yet if we see the serial killer as belonging not to the human species specifically, but to the animal kingdom in general, and as being similar to a lion, a hyena, a crocodile, or even as belonging to some otherworldly beast, we may then relinquish once and for all our need to explain his actions to ourselves. It is in the nature of a lion to kill. It is in the nature of a serial killer to kill—thereby acting out his specific animal impulses. We are not concerned with *how* a born human has ended up becoming a beast. This is a completely different matter. Here we are only concerned with how things *are* and how we view them.

Since Plato, many writers and philosophers have assigned animal characteristics to humans, as we do when we say someone "is a snake" or "eats like a pig." In such cases, we use metaphor to suggest a similarity, but we still maintain our view that the person in question remains a human. Yet, in as much as a human is an amalgam of disconnected and disparate behaviors that come together under a loose mental guidance, each person comprises many personas. Some of these personas may gradually develop into another being altogether. In such cases, the "transformed human" ends up resembling more the behavior of animals or imaginary beasts. Still though, bestial elements may actually coexist with benign characteristics in this new entity. Even serial killers are known to have been kind and loving to family, not to mention the many people they have decided not to kill, just as a lion is loving and kind to his own pride. When we radically shift the way we see such people, many so-called "mysteries" of human action vanish. The moment we cease to place a serial killer into the category of "human" (although externally he looks and might occasionally behave like one), we relinquish our need to understand him *as* human. Placing him in the mammalian order of carnivores and the family of hyenas, his actions cease to require any further understanding. Albeit residing in a human body, walking and talking, *he is* a hyena: his nature, to which he unwittingly succumbs, is to kill. He does not think and act; his thinking is simply subservient to his instinctive impulses. His actions are not that of a *moral agent*, but that of an animal succumbing to Nature.

We may even go a step further and completely devitalize both animals and the serial killer: the lion, the hyena, and the serial killer are *Nature acting spontaneously*, without a name, without any ethical rules. Function and behavior precede our definitions—name and form. Thus, the behavior of these living beings may be seen as something akin to a storm or a tsunami that may kill thousands with their blind might. A serial killer may then be viewed as an unusual *natural force*—inanimate, neutral, aimless, and meaningless. Like a tsunami, he too is carried by the blind forces that move the universe. Are we ever baffled by our inability to understand "why" a tsunami, an earthquake, or ... a pandemic acted the way it did? Nature is the way it is. Simply put: *there is nothing to understand.*

One may retort that the renaming of something we cannot comprehend does not really solve the problem of understanding, and that inhumane acts by humans still remain a mystery. This is partly correct. But we would in turn respond that this latter mystery is of another type. It is not the mystery of "why" anymore. We would never assert that there is a mystery in *why* a lion kills or an earthquake destroys—we know and understand why these things happen. The question is transposed to a more general and philosophical one: Why do lions exist that kill antelopes, and why do earthquakes exist that can bring so much destruction and death to living beings? This is almost an identical question to the *why of it all*: Why is our world the way it is? We then need not isolate the "why" of a serial killer, but incorporate it into the big overarching philosophical question of Life itself.

But the reason we preoccupy ourselves with the problem of understanding such "unexplainable" and extreme human behavior is not to substitute one type of mystery with another. It is not simply a philosophical or theoretical issue. It is a *practical* one. The most important reason for shedding light on name and form is to expunge the sting of our suffering. For a big part of our suffering is not suffering itself, but our inability to understand and explain it.

Applying this whole approach to our everyday life, we may start by viewing people as *beings of Nature* rather than as well-defined "humans" on which we subsequently attach our preconceived ideas of how they *ought* to behave. Thus, every human being becomes a strange animal, so to speak, whom we have to approach with both love and caution. There is no absolutely predictable human behavior, just as there are no absolutely predictable natural phenomena. Just as a tsunami may strike without warning at any moment, similarly (or more so!), a human being may react to any circumstance or to the behavior of any other human being in most unpredictable ways.

Acknowledging beforehand that it is one's behavior that defines one's nature and not the other way around, we may slowly begin to accept *the reality of the variation of real beings* that inhabit our world and cross our life's path. We may then stop trying to understand why a person is who he is and acts the way he acts, and instead accept that he is such as who he is and behaves such as he behaves. It is this acceptance of the *suchness* of the behavior of other people, an acceptance that goes beyond name and form, and which is identical to the suchness of Nature itself, that in the end affords us the only true understanding of human behavior possible to us: that there is nothing to understand.

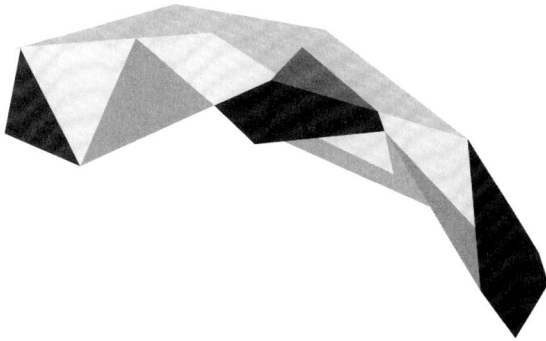

On the Modern World

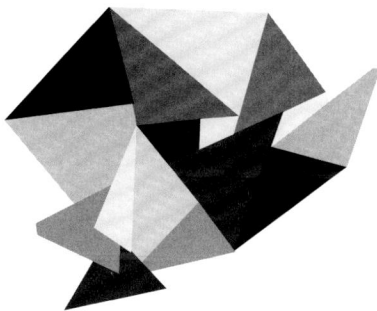

The Others' Gaze

The gaze of others defines us.

So long as we are alone, we do not have an outside view of ourselves to which we might refer; we exist within our inner being, which has no identity and no characteristics. But when others enter the picture, we suddenly obtain "an identity."

No other philosopher has spent so much energy studying the effect the gaze of others has on our life as the twentieth-century French philosopher Jean-Paul Sartre. He came to the conclusion that this gaze gives rise to a new kind of being, which he termed "being-for-others." Our sense of self and of how we view ourselves in society is inextricably linked to the way we feel another's gaze upon us. Sartre gives the example of someone who spies through a keyhole: suddenly, he hears footsteps down the hall and feels the gaze of another person on his back. At this moment, he ceases to be a conscious free being immersed in the experience of viewing, and becomes an object within someone else's world. He becomes a person with an identity—that of a voyeur. His being-in-itself (the term Sartre uses to describe the experience of pure being) becomes an object in the world, a being-for-others.

We need not go deep into Sartre's philosophy here to take this idea of the gaze and relate it to our everyday lives. I'm sure Sartre would have been elated to be living today, observing the behavior of people on social media, and discovering how well his theories have fared. The whole world has become the testing field for Sartre's theories. In the twenty-first century, most human beings not only strive to obtain the gaze of as many people as possible but define themselves in an almost absolute manner by and through that gaze. Suddenly, none of us need peep through keyholes: the lives of others, every little detail of what they do, is out there in the open. Just as is our own life that we voluntarily exhibit.

Now we are all not only voyeurs, but also exhibitionists.

The personal Facebook page becomes not a tool for self-expression, as many would have us believe, but rather the template upon which modern man strives to build his being-for-others. Unlike Sartre's voyeur, who was in the state of being-for-himself before he was caught (a mode of being with which he could still reconnect later), the modern individual willingly consents to surrender this permanently to "the multitude" (to use Seneca's favorite term). We all watch and are constantly being watched. And while we feel this gaze of others, we form identities and personas under the guiding principle of others' opinions, values, and (gossiping) interests. We consent to conform to what the multitude wants and expects from us so that we may have more Facebook likes, more Instagram followers, more YouTube views, more website visits. So, slowly but steadily, we end up constructing an artificial entity that we mistake for ourselves, an entity that lives and breathes and moves and acts, not for itself but in order to comply with what it understands as the desire of the collective gaze.

The woman who works out at the gym and uploads a dozen pictures of her toned body every day to the cheers and likes of her "followers" (the contemporary and infinitely more respected manifestation of Sartre's voyeur!); the young man who uploads prank videos; the professional who shares what he thinks would be liked by his peers—all unwittingly *create* themselves, or rather *a vision of themselves*, through the eyes of others. Through "posts" and "sharing," by exhibiting our loves and tastes, personal stories, photos, and more, each of us "curates" a public image of ourself to which we then continually strive to conform. Personal identity becomes our reflection in the eyes of others. One's being-on-Facebook (or YouTube or Instagram or TikTok) has become the ubiquitous reality of Sartre's being-for-others.

What is even more disturbing is that the being-for-others has begun to extinguish altogether the being-for-oneself (the equivalent of Sartre's being-in-itself). The modern exhibitionist, for whom all others are voyeurs, ends up being *only* this artificial and constructed being-for-others. Whatever he thinks and does and shares becomes permanently embedded in and thus guided by this gaze. The exhibitionist (who is also himself a voyeur) becomes permanently estranged from his own being. He exists only for the others' gaze; he is constantly preoccupied with this gaze, and works only for the preservation of his public persona. There is no "personal" anymore. No private life. No peeping alone through the keyhole. All is there for all to see. Most disturbingly: *what is seen by the world becomes what each person also sees in the mirror when he sees himself.* The others' gaze, but also their values, opinions, and judgments, become our own. We identify with the image others have created of us, and this image in turn guides our lives and actions. We come to believe that our Facebook or Instagram persona, our public image (with the comments underneath it) *is* who we are. Some even "peek through" their computer screens to see themselves as others see them, in order to be sure of who they *really* are.

In effect, they have become self-voyeurs!

They reaffirm their personal identity (or rather identification) by referring to their public image. The gaze of others defines them, and they accept this definition of themselves. In this way they are forever lost in the vast expanses of public space, where all is created and defined by the multitude.

What was first termed estrangement or alienation by the existentialist philosophers of the twentieth century has now become the reality of twenty-first-century man. Yet because this reality is all around us, or rather envelops us as we move in it, we do not see it. We are estranged in the midst of a greatly enlarged world, yet we do not know it, because the gaze (and clutter) of others keeps the wheel of our lives moving. We exist as long as we can keep others interested. This is what gives us our sense of identity.

Or rather, our multiple identities! For another offshoot of all this is that we have ceased to be a singular self. We create through the others' gaze multiple identities across digital platforms. We may become the humorous Facebook guy, the Instagram influencer, the serious LinkedIn professional, the playful YouTuber—all at once. If there was ever a hope of returning to our being-in-itself, to finding our center and our true freedom, now this is forever lost, for we cannot even conceive of our self as a singular entity. We are as many as the different groups of eyes that gaze upon us. We are all multiple personalities moving unconsciously in many different digital worlds … with a lost center and many faces.

The others' gaze lies at the heart of modern man's alienation. And the first action to take towards escaping its far-reaching effects is to stare back and discover the utter emptiness of this gaze.

The Era of Sound Bites

We live in the era of sound bites.

The overwhelming majority of our communication has been reduced to posts, tweets, text messages, and one-liners. Attention spans have dwindled, and argumentative reasoning has been reduced to "the final statement," which often is none other than the title of an article! Few have the mental energy to follow a complicated argument, to read a long and demanding piece of writing, a nonfiction book that may require engaging with ideas at some deeper level.

This spills over into our everyday human interactions too: many are not interested in listening to an elaborate intellectual discourse. Before you even start speaking, it is insisted upon that you provide a summary, the conclusion, the "main message" of what you have not yet uttered.

Content has now become the description of the content!

In the last few years, I have all the more frequently been hearing phrases like: "You don't need to explain it to me. Just tell me where you stand with respect to this." But my explanation—the way I think and reason—is the what, the how, the why, of where I stand. My final "stance" is less important than the mental process that led to it. The reasoning, the analysis, the "proof" is the real pedestal on which a person (and an idea) "stands." Otherwise, with one's opinion, values, reasoning lacking, one may as well copy what somebody else says, or simply choose at random between one of many different positions—akin to casting a ballot. But mindless voting is worse than not voting at all.

Although we live in the digital era where "engagement" and "interactivity" are meticulously studied and scientifically quantified, we are increasingly unable to *truly* engage and *truly* interact. Many make statements or post tweets, and have others similarly respond to those statements, without ever feeling obliged to explain how they came to think that way. The statements therefore remain hanging in a vacuum of presumably self-evident assumptions that they expect others to fill in. Yet, personal assumptions are rarely self-evident and even more rarely universal. Personal assumptions are, in fact, the individual mental scaffolding that needs to be defended as much as the edifice of the argument uttered. Such tweets and short comments that are supposed to be self-evident yet lack any foundation simply remain elements in a series of loosely connected jabber: statements forming endless threads that know not their whence and whither—a downward spiral of ephemera.

The era of sound bites is also the era of intellectual laziness. Phrases like "keep it short," "get to the point quickly," "too complicated, make it simple," are also an attempt to mask intellectual laziness. Many are not willing to mentally exert themselves, to truly listen attentively, to focus. For they have become used to being served easy sound bites that require minimal mental effort. This is even more common among our youth. There seems to be a ubiquitous lack of concentration. More and more people appear to have "attention deficit disorder"—they are scatterbrained.

Yet neither human communication, nor deep ideas, nor music, nor art, nor literature, can conform to this new universal obsession. The real world we live in is not a world of sound bites. Neither are some of the greatest human creations we all admire—whether it be a long musical composition, an elaborate philosophical theory, a mathematical proof, or, to use more everyday examples, a sophisticated French dish or a beautiful Japanese garden, each requiring many hours, if not days, of meticulous concentrated work to produce.

A very powerful moment from the movie *Amadeus* pertinently comes to mind. In the scene, the emperor, who is lacking in musical appreciation, feels like making a critical comment of some sort just in order to make a critical comment. So he tells Mozart, who has just finished conducting one of his operas, that the piece had "too many notes" and then elaborates further by adding, "There are in fact so many notes an ear can hear in the course of an evening." He then tells him to … "Just cut a few and it will be perfect," to which Mozart ingeniously replies, "Which few did you have in mind, Majesty?" The king becomes naked the moment he is challenged to elaborate on his strange idea, just as the tweeter or sound-biter will be truly revealed the moment he is challenged to engage on a deeper level.

Just as you cannot shorten a Mozart opera to make it more palatable to the untrained ear, similarly you cannot shorten a cinematic masterpiece to make it more digestible. Yet this is exactly what happened in 1984, the same year *Amadeus* was released, when the film distributors of Sergio Leone's magnum opus, *Once Upon a Time in America*, decided to shave off over an hour from the movie so it would fit the slots of movie theaters and be less "demanding" of the viewer. The movie did very poorly in the US, where it was shortened, but did well in Europe, where the director's cut was shown. Since the film's storyline spanned over half a century of New York's history through the lives of its protagonists, the movie's almost four-hour duration was imperative. Unfortunately, this movie was Leone's last, for he passed away a few years later—some say because of his sadness over the failure of his film in the US box office.

Now, thirty years later, Leone's magnificent creation is acknowledged as such, and its length is seen as an integral part of its message. It was the storyline that determined the film's length, just as it is the nature of reasoning that determines the length of a philosophical argument, and the nature of a writer's inspiration that guides the length of a poem or an essay.

It seems that the year 1984 is not brought into the discussion by pure chance: through a beautiful synchronicity, it also points to George Orwell's masterpiece. The novel *1984* describes an alienating totalitarian world of brainwashing and propaganda. As it turns out, all propaganda in Orwell's world is based on sound bites, ideas that are immediately understood and impress the mind without any effort. Yet for such propaganda to succeed, its recipients must already be passive, too lazy to think, and prone to simplistic, mass-produced ideas. The only way to resist any propaganda, therefore, is to challenge intellectual laziness, to fight against the lack of argument, the absence of proof and complicated ideas. Oppose, in other words, the descent into a world of sound bites.

The actual year 1984 did not bring with it the world Orwell had imagined. Yet because of the subtle connection between Mozart and Leone, each being asked to simplify his art, for me, 1984 marks the beginning of the Era of Sound Bites. Furthermore, the fact that this era began in the Orwellian year holds a hidden message: that the danger is not over, and that it may lie in something seemingly innocent and inconspicuous with which we are all becoming slowly accustomed.

There are times, as in advertising and in various political campaigns, when short messages and slogans are necessary and prudent. But when most human discourse is increasingly becoming sound bites, we need to be vigilant, and, quoting Dylan Thomas in another context, "do not go gentle into that good night, but rage, rage against the dying of the light."

The Digital Self

The other day I wasn't sure I existed. So I googled myself to be sure I did.

There was my face, my book, my speeches, my interviews, even "my quotes"—selected excerpts from my book on Goodreads.

I existed, all right!

For the first time in my life (and in human history), the search engines and data banks of the whole world—the digital libraries in which all knowledge and all things are registered—were corroborating my existence.

But this is a new type of existence. We experience Sartre's being-in-the-world not from within, but from without. This new being—let us call it our "digital self"—is sustained by the eyes that view it on the internet. The corroboration of the others' gaze is not simply one of the many aspects of living in society—as was the case for millennia. Today, it is the primary element, it is the one thing that makes our world *real*! Nothing we do becomes real until it has been posted in the public space; it becomes real by becoming digital. Descartes's *cogito ergo sum* (I think therefore I am) has become *ego vidisset ergo sum* (I am seen therefore I am). And Berkeley's *esse est percipi* (to be is to be perceived) has now become *esse est in internet est* (to be is to exist on the internet). These new realities are neither metaphors nor exaggerations. We are talking about a new *mode* of being—or rather, of coming-to-be! It's like a new birth. Each one of us is being reborn as *a new being* online.

But let us start from the beginning.

I have my social circles, my family, friends, many acquaintances, and the people I see every now and then, such as my local barber, the newsstand lady, the butcher, the dentist, and more. They know me by interacting with my body in physical space. There is intimacy, exchange of feeling, psychological nearness, physical contact. Until recently, these were the only real human interactions I knew existed. But now, this small circle of people who used to be the total number of people who knew me in the physical world has shrunk to almost zero. Now there is another huge set, a gargantuan circle that has completely dwarfed the previous group: the thousands of people who come to know my digital self on the internet. I seem to exist simultaneously in two parallel worlds—the old physical world where my physical body resides and interacts with others, and the digital world in which my new digital self has been born and is taking on a life of its own.

Just as these two selves are inseparable to others, they are slowly becoming inseparable to me! They mingle and occasionally merge in weird new ways, thereby creating a kind of a new composite self that partakes of both worlds. I observe that I have begun taking care of the digital self as I take care of my physical self, switching from one to the other as if they are two sides of the same coin. This caring-for has a digital term borrowed from the arts: curation. Most of us spend significant time curating our digital self. I have to choose one avatar for my YouTube self, a particular photo and description for my website self, another one for my Amazon self, and so on. I request hearts and likes and comments from friends or from this new group of digital friends called "followers." And having limited time to run after all these things, I occasionally recruit others to do the curating on my behalf. For just as you go to the barber to cut your hair, or the manicurist to groom your nails, there are now companies and freelancers who offer to help improve the image and status of your digital self: they boost your YouTube channel, give you likes and views, find you new followers, and offer a million other goodies of the digital world. Forget your diplomas and earned titles—these are the weights and measures of a bygone era! The era of Digital Flooding (see next essay) has already washed them away. The likes and upvotes, smileys and hearts, the number of followers and number of views—*these* are the new measures of one's standing in the digital universe, and by extension in the contemporary world at large. Of course, just as you can never know the complete character of a man from his perfectly coiffed beard, or the personality of a woman from her manicure, you can never know someone by these superficial digital metrics.

But how is this digital self actually constructed? What are the building blocks we use, and what are the guiding forces behind our curating?

There is a constant dialogue between four elements that come together: who we believe we are now, who we want to be in the future, how we think others see us now, and how we want them to view us. Out of this quaternity, these four "visions of ourself," we create our digital self. So this self may be said to capture *some* of the truth of who we are and what we want to achieve. But unfortunately, the others' gaze is so demanding, the judgment, opinions, and values of the multitude so pressing and influencing, that the last of the four elements—how we want others to view us—ends up overwhelming the other three. The social, the public, the shareable elements of ourself are much more important in the Digital Age because it is in the nature of the internet to filter everything so as to make it socially acceptable, publicly available, and easily shareable to a wider audience. Just as politicians direct the majority of their activities and discourse to the lowest common denominator of the multitude, the others' gaze on the internet makes us direct our digital curation to the masses. Therefore, our digital self, created in this way, ends up being as superficial and empty as the sweet-lipped political candidate who will say anything to attract voters.

But the digital self cannot wholly be understood and explored by these analogies. For when it is examined carefully, it is neither singular nor able to be delineated with exactitude. We recall the multiple identities of a previous essay: the social Facebook guy, the serious LinkedIn professional, the playful YouTuber. The simultaneity of these identities in itself need not be problematic. We can all already grasp and (consciously or unconsciously) accept the idea that we are not a singular self. And that we have different personas that we use according to where we are, what we do, and with whom we interact: we behave differently with our close friends than we do with the prime minister. Having one or more personas residing in digital space seems to be no different from simply adding a few more personas to the already rather large set we carry around in our offline life. The birth and curation of our digital self could therefore easily be dismissed as nothing truly serious. It could just be the new colorful and even playful "fashion" of the Digital Age. Or the natural outcome of the recent explosion in the ownership of mobile devices, which will simply pass as all fashions pass. Unfortunately, this is not the case. Not simply because—as we saw earlier—the digital self dwarfs the physical one, but mainly because, with its many personas, it does not remain contained in the digital universe: *the digital self overflows and spreads out into the real world where it messes with our life as a whole!*

Take the now ubiquitous scene of four young people sitting around a table at a café. They are absolutely silent, each holding their mobile phones, staring and tapping at the screen. They are all "in" the internet—in this other dimension of Being, where physical space, physical proximity, the real world with the sun's rays, city sounds, surrounding people all vanish completely. It does not matter where these four people are: they might as well be sitting at home or be situated on different continents! They are each "chatting" through their mobile screens with other friends who are not in the café. They send messages via Twitter, upload posts on Facebook and Instagram. Paradoxically, although they are with their friends in the café, they are not interacting with them. They are instead interacting with their followers, their Facebook community, or their absent friends—who are actually not "absent," because digital space transcends physical space. Being with the "absent-present" friends *in itself* is not bad. It is being with the absent ones *rather* than with the ones sitting next to them that is the problem. For it diminishes, if not cancels, the whole experience of "going out with friends." One may retort that there is nothing wrong with this, and that it is simply a new way of interacting with other people. But even if this is a new type of behavior, it is not a way of interacting but rather of *not* interacting! We cannot simply redefine what socializing is in order to include in it its opposite, i.e., non-socializing. Such unsociable behavior is a clear example of the digital self overflowing into the real world and messing it up.

But this is not all. The four friends do something that is even more unbelievable: while they are immersed in the digital dimension by texting absent friends, browsing their newsfeeds, or uploading posts, at some point they begin sending messages to one another *in the café*, thereby communicating among themselves via the internet! Suddenly, without leaving this other digital dimension, they are silently conversing with one another via the abbreviated phrases and sound bites that have replaced proper conversation, eye-contact, and, most importantly, *focused interaction*. Their attention is scattered about as they jump from one digital platform to another, exchanging messages and surfing the web. The word "surfing" is actually the most appropriate to describe the totality of the continual unsteady movements of such dispersed minds: it is surfing on the surface of waves—it is foam and froth and vapor! Furthermore, the friends also hug, kiss, send hearts, and do a hundred other things by typing graphics that merely signify these acts, neither glancing at one another nor moving an inch from their seats. They are all "acting out" simulations of real-life actions via the web. The real world has suddenly acquired a mirror image in the digital world, in which all human activities have become digitalized into a series of symbols. An entire range of emojis communicate actions that people would like to do (but don't!), such as hugging, kissing, laughing, screaming, congratulating. Other icons express human emotions (that people do not express!), such as love, boredom, sadness, and anger. No longer is there a need to perform any of these acts. The exchange of mere symbols has replaced the actions themselves, turning them into newly created digital acts that somehow pertain to both worlds: a digital hug creates in one's imagination the real hug, and then one imagines the hugging, thereby supposedly "acting it out digitally"—whatever that means! The four friends are talking with one another, hugging, expressing happiness, sadness, anger, and more via their mobiles, without even raising their heads to see one another. In this digital dimension, not only are we all without bodies, *but our actions and emotions seem to have been separated from our bodies.* We are becoming immobile typists who need no lips to speak or kiss, no arms to hug, no legs to visit places.

This incredible new reality brings to mind an episode of *Star Trek* in which the starship *Enterprise* falls upon a planet whose inhabitants are so much ahead of us in evolution that they have discarded all of their body parts. What remains of them are their naked brains in large glass fishbowls connected to machines. These brains only have to think of something to make it happen. Watching the young generation at the café, it is hard to shake the feeling that this is where our future civilization is heading. Today's typing fingers are already being replaced by voice recognition systems—there go the hands; in 200 years from now, we will connect our brains to programs that will read our thoughts so we won't even need to speak—there go the mouth and ears. And virtual reality will free us from the need to travel and visit foreign lands—there go the legs.

We are all moving towards our glorious future as disembodied brains!

The digital self, with its many curated personas, its new language and vocabulary, its digital simulations of human activity that are slowly replacing real actions, is now steadily and stealthily overwhelming our physical self and taking control of our lives. Our only defense is to observe, study, and understand it, so that we can try to contain it and force it to remain where it is supposed to live.

Digital Flooding

We have ceased to communicate, for we speak in sound bites.
We have ceased to be ourselves, for we exist for the others' gaze.
We have ceased to be original, for we conform to the multitude's demands.
Yet none is a more serious predicament than the fact that …

We have ceased to learn, for we have become obsessed with information.

We live in the Era of Digital Flooding. We are drowning in the infinite information available on our smartphones and digital devices. Like magicians, we touch a screen and the information comes flooding in. We are overwhelmed, mesmerized, dumbfounded. We don't know what to touch or click next, we don't know where to turn or what to make of all this. So we keep mindlessly searching and ceaselessly absorbing whatever this gargantuan parallel universe of information keeps throwing at us. By clicking one link after another, we often fall into a Wikipedia wormhole to find ourselves in some remote corner of an unknown galaxy, having forgotten our whence and whither! Yet …

Information is not learning.
Knowing facts is not learning.
Memorizing is not learning.

Learning is not the gathering and recording of information; it is the *ordering* of information. And ordering is not only sorting out, categorizing, and structuring: most importantly, it is finding the *meaning* of information, by interpreting and understanding it as well as by forming its *connections* with all else we already know. Learning is creating new mental pathways whereby the information has become meaningful and relevant to the rest of our knowledge and to the totality of our life.

For information to become useful, we must leave the field of information: understanding and meaning reside in a dimension that is outside of information itself! Just like the "Philosophy of Art," which belongs to the field of philosophy because it examines art from a distance, understanding and meaning lie *beyond* the information that is analyzed and interpreted. You may know a million facts about WWII, but do you know its causes? How it came to be? What were its consequences? How it relates to the peace that has followed it? It is the answers to questions such as these that constitute the true significance of all the events that have transpired in history. All true knowledge is the product of understanding, meaning, and the mental interconnectedness of information.

Many know everything there is to know about fashion, but they do not know how to dress themselves. Others know about the details of the latest theater or film productions, yet they have never attended a staged play or rarely go to the movies to appreciate a great film. What is the use of their specialized knowledge if it is unrelated to their lives as well as to Life itself? In the end, their knowledge is knowledge of subjects they neither really understand nor truly appreciate—such knowledge moves on the plane of superficiality and irrelevancy. Our contemporary world is full of such strange phenomena.

In 1803, when the owner's son took over his father's position, the *London Times* jumped from being four pages long (basically a huge folded sheet) to twelve. In an instant, it tripled the number of news items it could hold and added much more information across a broad range of subjects. Probably it is this that marked the beginning of the Information Age: rather than succeeding the Industrial Revolution, the Information Age appeared contemporaneously with the former and has been imposing its steady influence stealthily and gradually ever since. The *London Times*, with its multiple sections and free inserted magazines, is now hundreds of pages long—not to mention it has a continually updated digital edition.

The *London Times*'s evolution is most relevant to our discussion, for today's obsessive acquisition of information has become driven by *huge numbers*. The more information one is seen to gather, the more accomplished one seems to be to one's peers. The Blinkist app, one of many, embodies this truism: this app summarizes a book in a few pages, claiming one can "read" one hundred nonfiction books in a month. Of course, reading the summaries of one hundred books in a month is not reading even a single book! For all this fast "reading" is simply the stripping of understanding and meaning from the books. Suddenly, *all* books seem to exist for the gathering of information, not for learning or for the enjoyment of reading. Many young people growing up in this digital age cannot distinguish between information and knowledge. Many do not even know the difference between learning the technique of passing an exam and actually understanding the subject matter of their examination! Therefore, we have young people entering universities who have only a very superficial understanding of the subject they are about to study, although they may have mastered both the skill of gathering information as well as the "nascent craft" of passing university entrance exams. The percentage of people with university degrees has skyrocketed in the last few decades, but has the number of truly educated people increased with it?

The most disturbing phenomenon in all of this is actually the recent glorification of those persons who have become experts in memorizing tons of information and then displaying their "knowledge" in public. Popular television programs such as *Who Wants to Be a Million-*

aire, *Mastermind*, and *Jeopardy* are promoting the idea that those who are great memorizers and can keep in their short memory a plethora of useless information are to be admired and even rewarded for their special abilities. The skill of these people may be remarkable, yet the stealthily promoted idea that they represent the epitome of learning is not only utterly unfounded but, I would dare say, *dangerous*. For it suggests to the hundreds of millions who watch these programs around the world that these skills indicate that contestants are "well educated" and ought to be emulated. Yet the truth is much simpler, and even tautological: these people are simply good at winning TV shows—nothing more and nothing less. They may recall the exact date of a WWII battle, but ask them about the causes of WWII, and you will see most of them crumble.

The running after trivia is also clearly seen in another popular game of our times that supposedly tests the contestants' learning: *Trivial Pursuit*. The game, as its name suggests, is actually trivial in two ways: it promotes both the acquisition of trivial knowledge as well as the triviality of competing for it! In this context, Seneca's reference in *On the Shortness of Life* is as relevant today as it was two thousand years ago:

> It was once a foible confined to the Greeks to inquire into what number of rowers Odysseus had, whether the Iliad or the Odyssey was written first, whether moreover they belong to the same author, and various other matters of this stamp, which, if you keep them to yourself, in no way pleasure your secret soul, and, if you publish them, make you seem more of a bore than a scholar. But now this vain passion for learning useless things has assailed the Romans also. In the last few days I heard someone telling who was the first Roman general to do this or that; Duilius was the first who won a naval battle, Curius Dentatus was the first who had elephants led in his triumph … There will be no profit in such knowledge, nevertheless it wins our attention by reason of the attractiveness of an empty subject.

The number of Odysseus's rowers has simply been replaced with the number of the Kardashians' escapades!

But the most trivial of all is the myriad personal information that people share across social media. Digital flooding is at its highest on Facebook and Instagram, not to mention in the smartphone messages and photos and videos that we ceaselessly send one another. Parents are posting every single supposedly important event in their babies' lives … the first word, when she started walking, her first clever discovery. Many are busy uploading photos and videos, responding to comments, and then liking, sharing, posting heart emojis—they call this "communication," or "exchanging info," yet it is neither. People cannot interact with people anymore, only with the digital facades that people use to replace their real identities. These adopted personalities—or to use the modern word, avatars—in the end replace the real person himself and become superficial empty masks substituting the real character and soul of the individual.

There are a few who even document every single hour of their lives on social platforms, as if the whole world is interested in knowing when they eat and what time they go to bed. Of course, one obvious reason why such people insist on documenting their lives' trivia is that so many are willing to "follow" them and further encourage this behavior. The followers respond to trivia with trivial comments, which give rise to more trivialities, in a vicious circle that sustains itself through its own … inner power of triviality! The endless hours spent on such completely useless exchanges of information are taken from people's precious time that could have been invested in either true learning or true *living*. In a sense, we are all returning to our grandma's village of old, and are establishing a digital version of village mentality through which village gossip has reemerged on a global scale. The only difference from grandma's real village is that now it is not our neighbors' gaze that defines what we do and who we are, but the gaze of the whole world.

Nobody seems to know how to put the amazing gift of the infinite digital information that our privileged age provides us with to good use.

Nobody studies history nowadays, nor philosophy, psychology, sociology, geography, biology, astronomy.

Nobody reads serious books anymore—although more books are published than ever.

Nobody learns—all gather information.

Digital flooding is killing us.

Let's revolt!

On Busyness

Everybody nowadays is constantly busy. Moving around. Hectic. Carrying to-do lists that get longer and longer. Having errands to run, chores to finish, tasks to accomplish. Busy-ness, henceforth without a hyphen, has become the new ubiquitous reality in our modern world.

Christmas especially, and "holiday seasons" in general, for some strange reason that is difficult to pinpoint, always end up being periods of incessant activity. Instead of being what their name suggests—holidays, which mean a period of meditative calm, a time of rest and recuperation—they become the exact opposite. Most people spend an inordinate amount of time on shopping and moving about the city, planning, hosting friends or family, buying gifts, and sending and receiving greetings (most often from people who remember them once a year!), or even traveling to places where … everybody else is also traveling.

But busyness, although accentuated during holidays, is to be found throughout the year. It has actually become so prevalent in our times that the phenomenon is now even studied by psychologists. A 2016 scientific paper on the subject now claims that "busyness" is replacing conspicuous consumption (until recently the ultimate status symbol) as a public marker for one's worth.[10] A century ago, the ability to abstain from work and enjoy one's hobbies, sports, and travel, or simply to remain idle, was a symbol of nobility and status. But today, the whole idea has been completely reversed! In the twenty-first century, it is the busy person, or the one who simply *seems* busy or busyish, who is perceived as having high status. Interestingly, the same research demonstrated that wearing a Bluetooth headset, emblem of the busy multitasker, sends a stronger message about our social position than wearing a pair of standard headphones, which, being widely used for listening to music, rather suggest leisure and free time. As the article says, "Busyness and lack of leisure are also being more celebrated in the media. Advertising, often a barometer of social norms, used to feature wealthy people relaxing by the pool or on a yacht. Today, those ads are being replaced with ads featuring busy individuals who work long hours and have very limited leisure time." As it turns out, behaving in a way that shows one is constantly busy has become fashionable, and consciously or unconsciously, now … everybody does it.

As is often the case with research in the social sciences, this study describes and verifies a reality we have likely observed ourselves, but it does not explain how busyness has come about. Therefore, in trying to find the roots of this new phenomenon, we are on our own. So, we must leave descriptive sociology altogether and turn to the depths of human nature itself.

I think that busyness has its roots in something more substantial that goes beyond the dichotomies of high status vs. low status and work vs. leisure. Actually, busyness is not a synonym for hard work. Work is only part of it. *Busyness is a synonym for incessant activity, restless motion.* Its opposite is not sloth, but stillness. It is by discovering its

---

10 The findings of this research, titled "Research: Why Americans Are So Impressed by Busyness," by Silvia Bellezza, Neeru Paharia, and Anat Keinan, were published in the *Harvard Business* Review, December 15, 2016.

opposite that a new understanding is achieved: modern man requires incessant activity because he *fears* stillness.

But why is stillness frightful?

Stillness makes us come face to face with life's central themes: Who am I? Where did I come from? What am I doing here on this planet? What am I *supposed* to do? The moment we stop moving, and the sea foam on the surface of the water ceases to be our main preoccupation and is seen for the insignificant transient froth it is, we face the fact of the immense ocean of Life that envelops us and requests that we give a responsible response to these questions. Stillness makes us rethink the totality of our life; it incites us to reevaluate our life choices, what we do and why. Although we all need to struggle to come to terms with our incompleteness, we find the task daunting, and so we shrink back from it. And what do we do? We suddenly "remember" the bill we have to pay, and the toy we have to buy, and the email we have to send … and off we go.

Busyness becomes our existential comfort pill, the refuge from existential angst.

It takes the role of an external force that apparently does not allow us to sit still and think. But it is not external. It is the sea foam, or rather the smokescreen we ourselves *create* so that we may avoid facing the more important issues of Life itself. We shy away from the conscious suffering of development.

However, let us be honest and admit that not all people are preoccupied with the major questions of Life, or with the purpose or meaning of their lives, or even with "consciously developing." Let us also admit that not all *need* be preoccupied with such stuff. Who is to decide what each organism on this planet is meant to do? If so, then what's so bad about busyness? Especially if it can also impart the feeling of high status! Well, I think there are two negative aspects associated with busyness.

First, busyness is a license for irresponsibility, both towards others and towards ourselves: the most common excuse for why someone did not do something he ought to have done (or promised to do or committed himself to doing) is that he was "busy doing something else." But Life demands that we do what we ought to do, even if there are other things we also ought to be doing. One "ought" does not cancel another. Busyness as an excuse for leaving things undone has become even more commonplace than busyness itself. Suddenly, even the non-busy, aspiring to raise themselves to the higher status of both busyness and business, are *so* busy that they never finish their tasks. Nobody finishes anything anymore, because everybody is busy finishing "that other job." Of course, "that other job" is not finished either. Therefore, busyness becomes another name for that work that never finishes, as well as the excuse for *any other* work that never finishes. This also applies to all the jobs that we assign to ourselves. That's why it is also a license for being irresponsible towards ourselves. In the end, next year, we will not do what we vow to do—which is what we failed to do *this* year!—because we will be … just as busy. Our busyness is already the handy excuse for our future failure. The remedy for this endlessly recurring cycle is actually quite simple: it is knowing that you never *find* the time to do things; you *make* the time to do them. And to make time, you need only stop the incessant activity in order to *think of how* to make time.

The second, and much more important, negative effect of busyness on our life is best expressed in John Lennon's maxim from the 1980 song "Beautiful Boy," dedicated to his son: *"Life is what happens to you when you are busy making other plans."*

Such busyness has been around, on and off, for millennia, and although Lennon popularized the phrase, it was Seneca who first uttered it. The Stoic philosopher spent much time analyzing the idea in his writings. Seneca's most famous essay, "On the Shortness of Life," is actually in great part preoccupied with "the preoccupied," "the engrossed," "the busy"—as English translators have variously chosen to render Seneca's Latin term *occupatos*.

It is in this immortal essay that we also find the Roman version of Lennon's quote: *"You have been preoccupied while life hastens on.* Meanwhile death will arrive, and you have no choice in making yourself available for that."

At another point, we read: "Everybody agrees that no one pursuit can be successfully followed by a man who is busied with many things, since the mind, when its interests are divided, takes in nothing very deeply, but rejects everything that is, as it were, crammed into it. There is nothing the busy man is less busied with than living." What both Seneca and Lennon are saying is that busyness has the overall cumulative effect of disaster that *we ourselves* bring upon the totality of our life. Busyness estranges us from both Life itself and our own life in particular.

The most powerful passage expressing this alienation, again from Seneca, is the following:

> So you must not think a man has lived long because he has white hair and wrinkles: he has not lived long, just existed long. For suppose you should think that a man had had a long voyage who had been caught in a raging storm as he left harbor, and carried hither and thither and driven round and round in a circle by the rage of opposing winds? He did not have a long voyage, just a long tossing about.

What a great image that stays with you long after you have read it: busyness is none other than the "tossing about" of a helpless boat near the harbor!

Still, though, Lennon's poetic rendering is probably the most potent for modern man because of the ingenious way it is phrased: Lennon, like Seneca, tells us that Life itself does not *respect* our busyness. But instead of saying that life simply "hastens on," he uses a new verb that takes this idea to a new level: our life ends up "happening" to us in spite of us thinking we were doing something. Our doing is an illusion. For by being busy *doing* a million insignificant things, creating and then running after myriad errands or chores, inventing tasks and endless to-do lists to finish, our life *becomes* these things that we *do*. For our life is the totality of our *living*. The moment our living becomes a ceaseless busyness, it first ceases to be "ours," then ceases to be true living replete with beautiful moments, and finally it ceases to be a self-generated movement—it becomes something that seems to be imposed by some outside agent on us (hence the word "happens"). But it does not simply happen. It happens *to* us. The crucial word in Lennon's maxim is this "to." For it suggests a calamity, a disaster—reminding us of Seneca's helpless boat near the harbor. And what is this Lennonian disaster that happens to us?

We wake from our mechanical living after a few decades and realize that our life ended up being not the one we had envisaged, not the one we had planned, dreamed, and wanted, but one of incessant motion and activity, a never-ending busyness that although always seeming to be on the fringes of our life, a kind of intermediary stage in which we moved from one task to another, one postponement to another, somehow finally ended up being our whole life.

On Time

Time and Timing

Time is this grand, unfathomable, overwhelming entity we can never truly grasp. Mysterious and all-encompassing, it forever eludes our attempts to understand it. Even when we think we are near to grasping a part of its nature, we usually find it attached to some other entity that is more easily comprehended by us. In physics, we understand and study time only when it is related to space or motion; in philosophy, time has been understood to be one of the noetic categories through which we comprehend the world of phenomena; in psychology and neuroscience, it is related to our subjective modes of experiencing duration; in painting, it is suggested but never portrayed; in music, it is the basic building block of every composition.

Still, mingled as it is with other things, Time (henceforth with a capital T) has throughout the centuries been one of the symbols of the created universe itself. In the Vedas, Time starts the Creation and Time will one day end it: "From time all beings emerge, from time they advance and grow; in time they obtain rest." The same idea was entertained by the Christian theologians: unlike the Ancient Greeks (and Aristotle in particular, who thought that Time was infinite), Thomas Aquinas asserted that Time was born together with the Creation. For many philosophers and theologians, Time has always been this primal and monumental entity that, after it sets the World in motion, absorbs and destroys everything it contains. The Ancient Greeks identified it with the god Kronos, who ate his sons.[11] Simonides of Ceos called Time "*pandamator*" (πανδαμάτωρ)—which translates to one who consumes or subdues everything with his infinite power. Modern physics has the same view: Time will inevitably lead, via the Second Law of Thermodynamics and entropy, to the disintegration of everything.

We seem to have no control over Time. We did not choose to be born as humans in this era, we cannot stop our bodies from aging, we cannot return to the past and change what we did wrong, we cannot force the future to come earlier, we cannot stop the clock ticking. We are apparently powerless creatures *trapped* in the stream of Time, which is none other than the invisible expression of all change and all activity in the visible universe. We feel like little helpless ants moving about on the surface of a massive globe that rotates around a star situated at the edge of a galaxy.

Yet there *is* an escape from Time's suffocating tentacles!

There is something that mysteriously stands outside of Time, although at first glance it appears to be an integral part of Time, it seems to be entangled *in* it, and even its own name is derived from it: *Timing*.

Timing is the element that frees Man from Time. Not completely of course, for we are still carried around by Time's grand movement, and we will still age and die. But while being tossed and thrown about by the merciless god, we have the ability to rise above Time by choosing *when* to do what in our lives.

It is rare that a definition sheds any significant light on a complicated concept, yet the Oxford Dictionary's definition of "timing" seems not only to do just that but to somehow encapsulate all human experience and knowledge gathered throughout the centuries concerning

---

11 This is the same as the Roman god Saturn.

this term: *Timing—the choice, judgment, or control of when something should be done.* Those three nouns, themselves derived from three active verbs, seem to define not only freedom itself but its relationship to that mysterious power within Man called the Will. Choosing and controlling is willing, while judging is the ability to impose a rational or ethical order on the mechanical universe ruled by Time. Everything we do is situated in Time; yet, paradoxically, *the when* we do something is not!

The when we do whatever we do is dependent on the choice, the judgement, the control of our own Will.

And Time cannot touch it, although in Time our Will appears, in Time it acts, and through Time its results are manifested.

Timing is the measure of our ability to go over and beyond the "controlling circumstances" of our lives. Whenever we blame our inability to make an important decision in life on the things we apparently cannot control or on the momentum of our past choices (which in turn is another expression for Time's arrow running its natural course), we betray ourselves. For we relinquish our control over what we *can* control, which is our ability to act contrary to all controlling circumstances. In the end, the controlling circumstances are controlling us because we have willingly decided to become their slaves. The moment when we do something, when we act and do not remain passive in observing life take its own natural course, is the moment we impose our own human "law of the will" on Nature. Deciding upon the proper moment to act, and then actually acting, is the most important science and art Man ought to master. As we read in the well-known passage of Ecclesiastes 3:

There is a time for everything,
and a season for every activity under the heavens:
a time to be born and a time to die,

a time to plant and a time to uproot,
a time to kill and a time to heal,
a time to tear down and a time to build,
a time to weep and a time to laugh,
a time to mourn and a time to dance …

Being constantly mindful of Timing's central role in whatever we do is being mindful about our own unique and royal nature as humans—who possess Will and have the freedom to exercise it … at will.

But Timing is not just the great liberator from the little slaveries of everyday life. It does not only free us *from* Time; more importantly, it creates that part of our individual path *in* Time that does not belong *to* Time! Arthur Schopenhauer, who may be said to have brought together the highest creations of Western and Eastern philosophy (Kant and the Vedanta) in his magnum opus *The World as Will and Representation*, named Kant's "thing-in-itself" (the noumenon) as "Will." He did this on the grounds that the nearest we can ever come to having direct experience of the ungraspable noumenon's manifestations is through our own acts of Will, which allow us to experience the force and drive of the universe from within. Schopenhauer's Will was not, of course, identical to the human Will; it was a blind, purposeless, impersonal force. Still though, it is not insignificant that human Will brings us so close to experiencing in our very bones the transcendent substratum of the cosmos, whether we call it God, Nature, the One, or the Noumenon. As he writes:

> The act of the will is indeed only the nearest and clearest *phenomenon* of the thing-in-itself; yet it follows from this that, if all the other phenomena could be known by us just as immediately and intimately, we should be obliged to regard them precisely as that which the will is in us. Therefore in this sense I teach that the inner nature of everything is will, and I call the will the thing-in-itself.

And of all the acts of the Will, none is more important than *the when* we decide to act, the Timing of our actions. Timing is the point where Man meets with the Universe as an equal; where Time the destroyer encounters Man the creator; where the Laws of Nature are transcended by the human Will. If Time is the overwhelming entity that we have no control over and which we do not truly understand, Timing is the controllable entity of human dimensions that we know intimately through the act of willing.

There is nothing more *defining* in our lives than Timing. In Timing lies our sense of freedom and our willpower; our deepest grasping of both Time and Timelessness; our ability to create our individual path and to define who we are. If Time encloses within it disintegration, Timing continually creates through Man's Will the elements of harmony and order that together constitute our limited revolt against Time. If the inner nature of everything is Will, then the outer expression of this Will is none other than Timing.

At the Tip of Time's Arrow

Everybody alive today exists at the tip of Time's arrow, at the pinnacle of Being, the highest summit of evolution.

This Present, in which we exist at each and every moment of our lives, happens to be the most advanced point of the most advanced age in humanity's existence. Actually, this Present in which everything happens is *always and permanently* situated at this most advanced point. As one moment gives way to the next, it is replaced in turn with an infinite number of such endless present moments, all of which permanently reside at this forever recurring pinnacle of existence. Therefore, an equally amazing fact is that each and every human *who has ever lived* on this planet could also have thought of himself as living at the pinnacle of evolution! Subsequently, every human who will exist in the future will again exist at his own present moment, which will also exist at the tip of Time's arrow. The only constant substratum of everything in the universe is this Present at which everything *is* and *is becoming*. Generations upon generations of humans will come and go, but this Present will remain permanently immobile, "untouched by morning and untouched by noon."[12] Since each moment that passes by has no

---

12 From Emily Dickinson's poem "Safe in Their Alabaster Chambers."

effect on this Present, it might be conceived of as eternal. Everything I write now, but also everything you read at this moment, is always being written and read in an Eternal Present. Our lives and existence in general may seem to reside and move in Time, but this Time is nowhere to be found. What can be found is the Present, but this Present, being immobile, permanent, and therefore eternal, cannot be conceived or understood by our finite intellect—although it may occasionally be experienced by another faculty of our being. And though the Present cannot itself be contained in Time or located in Space, it contains everything that was, is, or will be. For one of its main "qualities," if we may be pardoned for using such a word to describe the indescribable, is that it is always "situated" (again an imperfect word) at the pinnacle of Being.

When one truly meditates on this idea, one realizes that even though each and every human ever to have lived on this planet existed at the most advanced age of humanity up to that moment, every subsequent generation still was more advanced, for it could "see" *more* of a past than each previous generation saw. Each generation rightly considers its Present as being the "most inclusive" of all pasts, even though this has been, is, and will be claimed, rightly again, by each generation past, present, and future.

The point at which we meet with Being is always the most advanced expression of Being.

Nobody ever existed in a "primitive past." Nobody ever knew himself to exist in the Stone Age, the Bronze Age, or the Middle Ages. Each and every human to have ever lived on this earth considered himself to be part of the most developed culture that existed up to that moment. It is only later generations that place the past in historical boxes with titles.

How does the realization of living at the tip of Time's arrow change the way we live?

First, we immediately become overwhelmed with a feeling of immense *responsibility*. Responsibility towards everything else that is now alive, everything that has made us who we are, and everything that will follow us. By being at the intersection of past and future, our responsibility extends in both directions: we need to be worthy of our ancestors and to create descendants who will in turn be worthy of us.

Second, we become conscious of the unique *power* deriving from the privilege of our present status. We know everything that our ancestors knew, plus much more. Despite his polymathy and great intellect, Aristotle knew less about our world and reality than today's average high school student. Meditating on this causes a major shift in our perspective. All the great discoveries of our ancestors are now part of our shared wealth. What was miraculous upon its invention, be it the steamboat, electricity, or the airplane, is now part of everyday commonality. There has never been an age so advanced—with computers, spaceships, medical technology, the internet, and artificial intelligence. There was never a time in history when any question posed by Man could be instantly answered by accessing the internet. The average lifespan has never been so long. Travel has never been so easy. Acknowledging these facts comes with the realization of an immense power never before held by Man, a power that ought to be used prudently. We, the imagined demigods of our ancestors, can, with this unique power, create new forms of society, new wondrous objects, expand our field of understanding, mold an even more advanced mental and spiritual being.

Third, we become *grateful* for being now alive at this pinnacle of evolution. Everything we are, everything we have and enjoy, everything we know and understand, is more advanced, more developed, more expansive than ever before. There has not been a more extraordinary world than ours. Let's rejoice every morning when we wake up, and let us begin our day with these words: "It is 2024. This advanced age has never before existed. And I am here, now, alive, belonging to this incredible world that was created for me to enjoy."

These three—responsibility, power, and gratefulness—must work in tandem and harmoniously complement one another. Let everything we do be permeated by the realization of our default and extraordinary position at the tip of Time's arrow, at the summit of evolution. And let everything we do be the result of power exercised responsibly and with gratitude for the opportunity we have to form an even better future than our privileged present.

Heraclitus's Unseen Waterfalls

Ever since Heraclitus, in the sixth century BCE, uttered his famous phrase *ta panta rei*, which means "everything flows" or "everything is in constant flux," humanity has accepted Change as one of the fundamental laws that govern the cosmos. Heraclitus's example of a continuously flowing river that can never be entered twice—because it is never the same river—has even become the archetypal image of this constant flux that permeates everything.

However, while the image of the river works most of the time, it is not all-inclusive and may actually be limiting or even misleading. For unlike the steady flow of change that the river suggests, change in the universe and in life also follows another pattern, one that is not smooth, steady, continuous, but rather abrupt, jagged, staggered.

In the physical world, the perpetual motion of elementary particles is not smooth, but "rugged." Particles move along a regular trajectory for some time before suddenly jumping into another type of movement, another level of energy. In the field of quantum mechanics, these abrupt changes have been termed "quantum jumps" and are one of the pillars of modern physics. What we considered for millennia to be the regularity of change in the physical world has been qualified by a new concept of Change that includes sudden movements.

The pattern of constant, uniform motion, broken suddenly by an abrupt movement, is also to be found in another science: biological evolution. When scientists began to closely study the fossil record in the second half of the twentieth century, they discovered a strange phenomenon: once a particular species appeared in the fossil record, it would become stable, showing little evolutionary change for most of its geological history. Then, after millennia, it would abruptly change form and either become a new species or acquire many new features. This observation led to the creation of the evolutionary theory of "punctuated equilibrium," which has now replaced the idea that evolution occurs uniformly, i.e., by the steady and gradual modification of organisms. According to the new theory, organisms stay in stasis or "equilibrium" for millennia and true evolution happens only in bursts of rapid change that "punctuate" this stasis. Based on these new discoveries, the latest theory, quantum evolution (borrowing the name from the now ubiquitous physics term), makes the bold claim that *all* grand evolution happens *only* in quantum jumps.

Moving from the grand evolutionary movement of biological organisms to the single life of an organism itself, we observe similar behavior. An often-used example in self-help literature is that of the Chinese bamboo that develops its root system over a period of four years only to suddenly grow shoots that pop up from the ground and grow over twenty meters tall within just six weeks. In many other plants, similar periods of constant and slow movement are punctuated by sudden accelerated activity that seems magical. In the animal kingdom, another often-used example—which in the East is also used as a symbol of spiritual transformation—is the lifecycle of the butterfly: we first have the caterpillar, which for a long period of time just eats incessantly and becomes fatter. Then, suddenly, it starts consuming its own body, turning into a chrysalis, from which later emerges a butterfly. The lifecycle of the butterfly, just as the grand movement of evolution itself, consists of stages of equilibrium punctuated by sudden bursts of transformative action.

Coming to Man himself, and to the field of human psychology, we have Jung's theory of the stages of life: childhood is broken by the sudden adolescent crisis that prepares one for adult life; then adulthood is in turn disturbed at around the age of forty by a midlife crisis that prepares one for the main adult period; and finally there is the late-life crisis at the onset of old age. Each constant phase of life is broken abruptly by a period of turmoil, stress, and sudden transformation, which becomes the existential fire that consumes the previous "stasis" in order to prepare a new life on another level.

Even in the field of history, we discover hundreds of examples that follow a similar pattern. The flourishing of great civilizations seems to happen at specific nodal points that are akin to revolutions: the sudden appearance of agriculture, followed by the creation of large cities over a very small time period; then the revolution of cavalry and the rapid movements of peoples and tribes across the steppes; then the flourishing of great civilizations in a short period of time. The classic civilization of Ancient Greece spanned only eighty years—yet again as if in a sudden burst of energy. At about the same time, Taoism and Confucianism appeared in China, creating a huge leap that would define Chinese civilization for millennia. And in modern times, we have, to name a couple, the Renaissance and the Industrial Revolution, in which we saw a rapid advancement in European civilization over a very short time span. Even political events seem to follow this pattern of steady continuity disrupted by violent upheavals. One recent example is the turbulent Communist Revolution in 1917, which led to a quite stable and steady period of communist rule, which in turn collapsed in 1989 due to sudden social turmoil.

Similar effects have been observed in economics, epidemiology, and more. Terms such as "critical mass" or "tipping point" have been used to describe processes at which sudden changes increase dramatically after a certain threshold is crossed.

All these examples from many diverse fields seem to suggest, if not actually *prove*, that Change in all observable phenomena happens in sudden bursts that break the default constant flux of Change itself. It seems that one needs only to follow the smoothly moving river of Heraclitus, walking alongside its bank, in order to discover a little bit further down that the river becomes a waterfall! Heraclitus's ceaselessly flowing river, signifying change and flux, is not merely one of constant, regular flow, but one that includes a variety of changes that disrupt the flow, creating new types of movement: not only waterfalls, but streams splitting into two or entering into a pond to reemerge flowing in another direction. We could even go a step further and suggest that the constant flow of the river—*any river of Change*—is but the field of preparation for a sudden change. In other words, the river does nothing but prepare the beautiful explosion of the waterfall, just as the quiet and slow transformations of the caterpillar and the chrysalis are the "field of preparation" for the magical flight of the colorful butterfly.

But why does Change follow such a pattern?

The answer to this may actually be quite simple: *everything being in constant flow means that the flow itself is in constant flow!*

Change is not immune to Change itself. If everything changes, then Change itself must also change. What we experience and observe as the disruption of uniform constant change is none other than the expression of the lurking change within Change: *the quantum jumps are but the disruptions of Change, which cannot remain unchanged, because it too obeys the law of itself.* If Change were predictable, then it would have become synonymous with regularity and stasis. The *unseen waterfalls of Heraclitus*, lying further down the river, are the symbol of the Change inherent in the flow of Change itself. It seems that Change cannot even "withstand" its own *constant and regular* change! It "needs" to create disruptions in its constancy, unpredictability in its mode of change, by changing the nature of itself. It is for this reason that Change, exactly because it itself changes, can never be captured, nor completely be understood, nor, of course, be predicted. We can never be certain, as we ride the river, when the next waterfall will appear and from what height we may fall, nor whether it will be a single waterfall that we find, or multiple small ones, or something else. Although change itself may sometimes be predicted to some measure, the change of Change will forever make all of our predictions uncertain.

But what is the practical significance in our lives of this law of the inconstancy of Change?

Knowing firstly that the law of change exists, and secondly that it self-modifies so that this change is punctuated by sudden rapid changes, we must become vigilant to these upheavals in order to be able to accommodate them in our personal lives when they do appear. "Vigilant" here means recognizing the periods of abrupt changes as such and boldly adapting to them by abandoning the familiar normal flow we have grown accustomed to. Unlike the commonly held belief popularized by the New Age movement and the recent emphasis on positive thinking, "going with the flow" does not necessarily mean flowing along the smooth regular river of change, but being ready, when on a cliff or precipice, to plunge into the sudden void and follow the waterfall to the next level. Sometimes "going with the flow" means recognizing that the flow is about to accelerate, slow down, or even reverse its course altogether; it may also mean putting up a good fight, standing your ground, or taking a hammer to the Berlin Wall—rather than staying home to watch events unfold by themselves on television. The flux itself being in constant flux means that we must also be ready to occasionally move in the opposite direction from the one in which we had been moving—to depart from the known path to follow the road less traveled.

Missing such junctures of sudden change, which usually happen when things in our life are "ripe" for a new series of rapid transformations, may mean that we miss one of the greatest gifts the Law of

Change has to offer us. For as we have seen, all major leaps in inanimate matter and living organisms in general, as well as in Man and human society in particular, seem to happen at these sudden quantum jumps, these junctures at which Change itself becomes "jaded" with its own regular movement and seeks to introduce major transformative action to engender new possibilities in the cosmos.

The law of Change demands from us that we never remain still, never stay too long in one place doing the same things. "For to stay [put] … is to freeze and crystallize and be bound in a mould," as Kahlil Gibran so eloquently put it. The Grand Law of Change demands that while we do change—and we can never force Change to cease—we must not remain complacent in our own change but welcome even more abrupt, revolutionary, bold, creative, strange and unusual changes that will take us to new levels of activity and life. Otherwise, if we are too slow to see the signs of the major shift that invites us to be a part of it, we risk missing the opportunity to evolve … from a reptile into a bird!

Let us always be mindful, not only of Heraclitus's forever flowing river that symbolizes the Law of Change governing the universe and our lives but also of the unseen waterfalls scattered within Change itself. These waterfalls actually reveal the grandest law of them all: the Law of the change of Change.

The Eternal Ragpicker

Truly, we do not think, will or act but thought occurs in us, will occurs in us, impulse and act occur in us; our ego-sense gathers around itself, refers to itself all this flow of natural activities. It is cosmic Force, it is Nature that forms the thought, imposes the will, imparts the impulse. Our body, mind and ego are a wave of that sea of force in action and do not govern it, but by it are governed and directed.
— Sri Aurobindo, *The Synthesis of Yoga*, Chapter VIII

❖ ❖ ❖

Your life is not really your life.

It is spread out, scattered around the cosmos. It was there before you were born. It is there—all of it—at the moment of your birth.

It is there in the fairy tales you grew up with, in the ancient plays and novels of your adulthood, in the poems that touch you deeply and to which you always return. You are Andersen's ugly duckling searching for your niche; you are *that* boy in the Emperor's New Clothes pointing to the naked king. You are Odysseus struggling to successfully steer your way through the fatal enchantments of life's Sirens. You are all these before you are all these. And once you become them, you realize that you always were them.

You are one of "The Souls of Old Men" of Cavafy decades before you become old. You are Oedipus Rex in the eternal tragedy of being, unraveling the tragic events you yourself unwittingly created; you are Prometheus bound, unjustifiably being punished by the gods for doing what they themselves decreed to be your highest duty; you are Arjuna, continually forced to choose between two equally noble paths.

You think you *create* your life, but when you look closely you realize that you actually *collect it* from the countless stories and myths, ideas and circumstances, the ordinary and extraordinary human lives that envelop your being. *You are a ragpicker of many lives!* You collect items as you go, sometimes lovingly and with care, at other times forcefully, succumbing to the law of necessity. And you put them in your own unique cart, forming a new life out of the inexhaustible variations of the myriad mythical or real, archetypal or time-bound lives in the cosmos.

The chapters of your "own" life are not really your own. They are timeless chapters in stories that are being played eternally. You are part of the eternal *unveiling* of Life itself. Or, rather, "Life's longing *for* itself."[13] Your life is not your *own* life because it is not *owned* by you. It "comes through you, but it belongs not to you." Your mortal frame is like a prism through which the light of Life enters in order to come out dispersed, not into a few component colors but into many variations of newly created activity, new forms of movement and creation and emotion and energy. You think you own both the prism and all the movements that come out of it. But in reality, you are neither the prism nor the movements. You are in a constant flux; you *are* the flux. You are the constantly changing aggregates, the five skandhas of Buddhism: you are a material form that ages and slowly disintegrates; you are a

---

13 From *The Prophet* by Kahlil Gibran.

chaotic amalgam of transient feelings and perceptions, of sensations and ideas. You have an identity that can never be captured, for it is ever-shifting; all that can be apparently captured is the various colors that you observe passing through the prism with which you briefly identify. It is through these transient identifications that you become an "I," an idea of a self that is a little point in space and time, with a body and a mind.

Yet exactly because your life is not your life, it is much larger than it seems. It extends beyond its spatial and temporal confines, beyond this little speck of moving flesh that seems to have appeared from nowhere and "knows not its own birth and end and cause."[14] Your life is part of the infinite powerhouse of the cosmos, part of the ceaseless and ever-renewable creative act, or rather *constant action,* of the Creation.

When you first began to "understand" this world, you were under the impression that you were creating a unique vision of a personal life, that you were molding and directing your life through your own actions. But it was not you who did that. It was another Force: the same Force that created you, that gave you this body and sensations and mind. You are but a "conscious Doll pushed a hundred ways" that "feels the push but not the hands that drive."[15]

But do not hasten to conclude that you are a mere nothingness! On the contrary: exactly because you do not own your life, you cannot lose it. And because it is collected from all these other lives, and therefore becomes a *resultant* of many lives, it is rooted in the principle of Life itself that can never be ejected out of Creation. It is because this life of yours extends beyond your personal little life and touches the universe at countless points that it has a strong footing in Eternal Being.

You *are* the protagonist of your beloved fairy tales and stories and

---

14 From Sri Aurobindo's *Savitri.*
15 From *Savitri.*

myths and poems. You *are* all the heroes you strive to emulate. You *are* all the lives you collect. Not only *are* you, but you always *have been*.

You are the forever reappearing Eternal Ragpicker of lives.

Destination Earth

A New Philosophy of Travel by a World-Traveler

by Nicos Hadjicostis

"Making the world his friend, considering it a single country, and then distilling from years of first hand experience a philosophy of travel, Nicos inspires and equips his readers not only to maximize the experience, but to maximize the value of the experience."
– Rick Steves, Travel Writer and TV Presenter

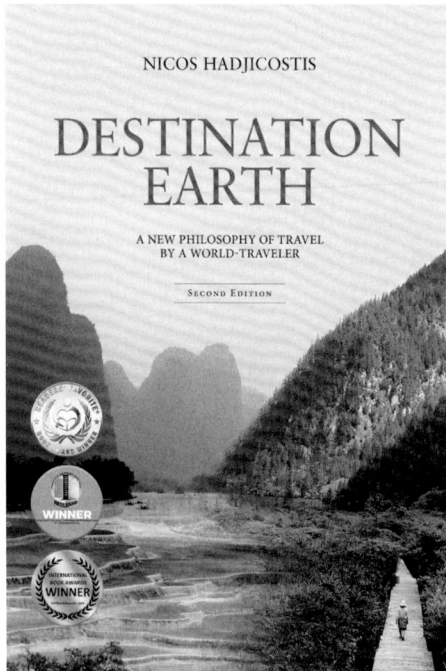

An award-winning book, *Destination Earth* provides a philosophical framework for embarking on more meaningful and purposeful travels. Inspired by the author's unique 6.5 year continuous around-the-world journey, during which he visited 70 countries on 6 continents, *Destination Earth* includes personal travel stories and color photographs from various places around the world.